MAKING CLASSIC
COUNTRY
CHAIRS

PRACTICAL PROJECTS COMPLETE WITH DETAILED PLANS

DAVID BRYANT

B. T. BATSFORD · LONDON

TO MY WIFE

I would like to express my sincere thanks to all those who offered help and guidance in the preparation of this book. I am particularly in debt to the following who allowed me to measure up many of the chairs featured in the book: The American Museum in Britain for the Bamboo Windsor chair; Harold Groom for the north west spindle-back chair; Peter Stone for the East Anglia hollow-seat chair; and Arthur Baker for the William Morris chair. I owe especial thanks to Dr. Bernard Cotton and the High Wycombe Chair Museum for their kind offers of help on chair-making matters, and for permission to feature the hollow-seat stool and the West Midlands corner chair from the 'Cotton' collection. Also, thanks are due to Don Whiting for help with early chair-making tools; Geoffrey Heath for the pictures of his leg trimmer and lathe drilling jigs; Alan and Marie Percival for assistance on photographic matters; and Robert Shepherd for assistance with drawing plots. Finally, my thanks go to my wife and family who supported me with much patience whilst I was working on this project.

First published 2001 by B T Batsford Ltd,
9 Blenheim Court
Brewery Road
London N7 9NY
Text, designs and black and white photography © David Bryant 2001

Colour photography by Keith Hewitt and John Coghlan

ISBN 0 7134 8040 8

Printed in Spain

CONTENTS

TECHNIQUES

PROJECTS

PREFACE

This book on country chairs is about how to make 'common vernacular seating' of the 18th and 19th centuries. It is divided into two parts, the first being a general introduction to chair-making techniques, and the second the design and construction of fourteen different chair projects, drawn from various regions of Britain and America.

The techniques section begins with a discussion on country chairs of the period 1750–1900 and briefly explores the different regional chair styles in Britain and America. I have then turned to the practical aspects of chair making using current skills and techniques. On woodturning, I have looked especially at the making of cabriole legs, which is necessary for some chair designs. The need for various jigs, essential if you are to guarantee success in chair making, is one of the most important aspects. I have devoted a chapter to a number of these jigs, many of which are adaptations and improvements on what others have done before. Another aspect of chair making covered in some detail is steam bending of wood parts, including slats, back posts and spindle work. On the practical side I have included details on seat weaving, which briefly covers the rush and tape weaving necessary for the designs in this book. A short piece on glues, finishing and basic chair assembly ends the techniques section.

In the second section of the book I have detailed a wide range of designs. Most of the chairs are measured from original period pieces and in some instances these are of provenanced origin. In the design drawings I have preserved, as far as possible, the original dimensions, though in certain instances minor modifications have been made. In general, each design is prefaced with notes on the history and evolution of the particular chair. The design drawings are in sufficient detail for the reader to be able to make a facsimile reproduction.

The designs of British regional chairs include a square back Windsor from the Thames Valley, rush-seated spindle and ladder-back chairs from the north west and Midlands area of England, and from East Anglia a hollow-seat chair typical of the Norfolk area. I have also included two designs for regional style stools, and an attractive William Morris armchair from the Arts and Craft Movement. Among the American designs are a bamboo-style Windsor from Massachusetts, a Shaker side chair and a rocker, a platform rocker and a child's slat-back chair with painted decoration. Two of the designs do not need turnery skills, and are included to show that you can produce attractive vernacular seating even if you do not possess a lathe.

Finally, I hope that this book will prove an inspiration to all who are interested in chair making. If you want to learn more on country chairs generally, then I would recommend without hesitation that you join one of the societies listed in the appendix and visit museums related to chair making.

David Bryant
Knutsford 2001

CHAPTER ONE
CHAIR MAKING

When we talk of country chairs we suggest by implication that these were made only for use in the country, which is rather misleading. Of course the type of chair we mean was not necessarily made or used solely by the country dweller, but was also produced for use in towns and cities all over the country, sometimes in quite large quantities. The word 'vernacular' is a slightly better term, meaning 'of one's native country', but even this is not truly what we have in mind. What we are really thinking of is not the expensive classic chairs by designers such as Chippendale, Sheraton and Hepplewhite made for the wealthier clientele, nor the mass-produced upholstered chair, but 'common seating' of regional origin made for ordinary people, for everyday use at affordable prices.

These country chairs made by individual craftsmen, small family concerns, and groups of chair makers working together to provide a living for themselves during the eighteenth and nineteenth century, fall broadly into two categories. The first are chairs with solid wood seats where the legs and back splat are fitted into this in dowel holes drilled in the seat board. These are called Windsor chairs. The second are those where the chair and the seat is built as a framework of adjoining rails and spindles, and the seat area is infilled with various materials such as rush and cane. Chairs with framed seats can also be infilled with wood planking (e.g. East Anglia hollow-seat chair – see later). However, these are not Windsors because the planking does not serve to carry the legs, back frame or any armrests.

REGIONAL CHAIRS IN BRITAIN

A study of common vernacular seating in Britain during the period 1750–1900 reveals, not unexpectedly, that distinct regional styles developed in different areas. The Windsor chair-making tradition, for example, developed in the Chiltern Hills and eventually focused on High Wycombe as the centre for production. Windsor chair-making also spread to the south west into Devon and Cornwall, and to the north east in Nottinghamshire, Yorkshire and Northumberland. There are a wide variety of Windsor chair types, which are essentially of two forms, either hoop- or square-back form, and with an intimate knowledge of styles it is possible to tell with reasonable certainty from which area one might have come.

In the north west of England chair makers produced a very different style of chair. These were rush-seated framed chairs with spindle and slat backs of varied patterns. A particular style of slat-back chair made in Cheshire and Lancashire was the so-called 'wavy line' slat back, which once seen is never forgotten. Some slat-back chair makers connected the top of the back posts with a curved strip of wood. These are known as 'bar-top' chairs. The town of Macclesfield, for example, is particularly renown for bar-top chairs made by the 'Leicester' chair-making family who worked in the Chestergate area. The bar-top tradition also spread to the adjoining countries of Staffordshire and Shropshire, and they are also recorded in Lincolnshire. Further north in the Lakeland counties another regional style of 'Dales' spindle-back chair evolved.

Moving south to the West Midlands counties of Worcestershire, Herefordshire and Shropshire a further chair-making tradition evolved. Here Philip Clissett, a well-known nineteenth-century chair maker, was in business at Boswell near Ledbury, along with other contemporaries such as the Warenders, Coles and Kerrys. A particular feature of their spindle and slat-back chairs was the thin flat plank seat board, which was rebated into round form seat rails. The spindles and stretcher styles were also uniquely different to other regions of Britain.

Over in East Anglia chair makers were making another altogether different style of chair from square section timber with slightly hollowed thin plank seats and tapered-form legs. These were essentially joiners, chairs as little or no woodturning was involved, and the back splats often incorporated Chippendale, Hepplewhite and Sheraton features of simplistic design. Further down in Suffolk, another regional chair style developed known as the Mendlesham. This is a form of Windsor with a thick wood seat with a square stick back with a middle splat. It often featured inset 'button balls'.

AMERICAN CHAIRS

In the United States vernacular seating developed in a uniquely American way. For example, the Americans developed the banister-back chair, so called because of their similarity to stair banisters. This was fitted with split-turned spindles with the flat side facing forward. It was at the height of popularity between 1700 and 1725. Windsor chairs were also made in large quantities as in Britain, but the woods used were different and often paler. Consequently American Windsors are mostly painted. One style attributable to the United States is the so-called bamboo Windsor where the spindles are turned with rings to simulate the effect of this Far Eastern timber. The period between 1800 and 1835 is particularly noted for fancy and painted chairs, with hand-painted and stencil decoration of increasing complexity as time passed.

The Americans also had a strong passion for rocking chairs of all manner of designs which primarily evolved during the nineteenth century. Before 1800 a rocking chair was more likely to be an ordinary chair that had been adapted with stuck-on rockers. A particular American innovation was the platform rocker developed during the second half of the nineteenth century, where the chair was attached by springs to a fixed base or platform and had an upholstered seat. In between all these we have the chairs produced by the Shaker movement at several settlements in New England from 1790 to 1900. This was a refined form of slat-back chair with a wood splint or tape woven seat, and was in essence a simplification of the earlier New England slat-back chair. These had varied forms of pommels, back slats, rockers and armrests and from a detailed knowledge of these you can tell from which settlement the chair might have come.

EARLY ENGLISH CHAIR MAKING

In the early days much vernacular chair making was done in woodland areas, with makeshift covers and small forest workshops for protection in the event of inclement weather. There being no electricity, chair making was essentially handwork, and the tools needed were consequently somewhat different to those we use today. Axes, mallets and saws of various types were used to split the tree trunk into manageable pieces (Fig 1. 1). A shaving horse (Fig 1.2) was used to work on small parts of cleft timber being trimmed with draw knife, and a pole lathe (Fig 1.3) was used for woodturning the spindle`work in the green. The lathe made up of a few bits of timber nailed or pegged together, with provision to hold the work between two fixed centres, was operated by a foot treadle. To work on larger boards, such as Windsor seats, an adze and an inshave were commonly used (Fig 1.4). These simple tools and devices were easily set up in a forest clearing.

Today the situation is very different, and chair making has moved into the factory environment. The fortunate craftsman working from home will have a dedicated workshop, but more often the garage is converted for this use. Nowadays we purchase our wood directly from a saw mill or timber yard,

Fig 1.2 Shaving horse.

Fig 1.3 Pole lathe.

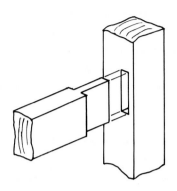

◀◀ Fig 1.4 Using an adze.

◀ Fig 1.6 Mortise and tenon jointing.

which the forester has converted into suitably seasoned planks ready for our use (Fig 1.5). We still use hand tools quite often, but in recent years the proliferation of electrically driven machinery, such as woodturning lathes, bench drills, planer thicknessers and so on, has taken much of the chore out of cutting and shaping timber to the form we want.

Skills and techniques

To make a chair requires a variety of different skills. They all utilise joinery in some form or other, but the range of chair styles that you can make using only square section timber and mortice and tenon connections is not great (Fig 1.6). Some 90 per cent of vernacular chairs require woodturning skills often for a large part of the construction. This is mostly spindle work and occasionally faceplate work perhaps for a stool top. Additionally, the chair maker needs staining, finishing and seat-weaving skills, which are not difficult to acquire given practice.

Tools and equipment

With regard to the tools necessary to make country chairs, I have assumed the reader has a reasonable complement of hand tools, including a hand plane and a selection of chisels. You will also need a suitable bench equipped with a strong vice. In addition, a medium-sized woodturning lathe is needed, and a bench drill is also recommended. With regard to cutting the hollowed form of a Windsor seat, a travisher is an effective tool for doing this (Fig 1.7). This is a form of spokeshave with a curved blade worked in a similar way and which is quite easy to use. Another tool developed in recent years for forming the long, thin spindle work on stick-back chairs is the rounder (Fig 1.8). This has a light alloy casting with two handles fitted with an adjustable spokeshave blade. As the rounder is worked along the slowly rotating square stock, it peels off the wood to form a spindle behind. Stick backs would otherwise be difficult to turn on a woodturning lathe because of their slender nature. On some

◀◀ Fig 1.5 Mobile bandsaw, used for planking a tree trunk.

◀ Fig 1.7 Hollowing a Windsor seat with a travisher.

rounders one of the handles has an adjustable grip so that you can taper down the end of a spindle.

Jointing jigs

One of the difficulties in joining chair parts together is in machining the mortice slots and dowel holes in the legs and back posts. You can cut mortice slots by hand and to some extent drill dowel holes by eye but this is not easy, and I have spent some time in my workshop developing simple jigs to make this simple. A section of this book covers the design of these. They are not difficult to make and you will be well rewarded by spending a little time making these up before you start. Once you have them you will find them invaluable for all sorts of other uses.

Steam bending

One aspect of chair making that continually crops up is the subject of steam bending. This is a skill needed for chair making that many try to avoid because it seems so difficult. For me much of the skill is self-taught, though I have tried to build on the work of others. In a separate chapter I have covered this in easy steps, from bending slats, to back posts and spindle work, and developed simple jigs to enable you to do this. The objective has been to make this easy for you to understand and do. I have briefly discussed the bending of Windsor hoop backs, although there are no designs in this book that require this skill.

WOODS

As far as wood is concerned I am not going to discuss in great detail the properties of different chair-making timbers that you can look up in specialist books covering this topic. Instead I will summarise those timbers that you will find on different types of vernacular chairs, and which are therefore appropriate to use for the projects in this book. These are the woods that are indigenous to Britain and America. As you would expect those used for making common seating in the past were largely dependent on wood that was available in the region in which the chair was being made. Woods that you will find in early British country chairs are summarised below.

Ash (European)

European Ash is an excellent wood for chair making and was very widely used for spindle and slat-back chairs c. 1780–1840. It is found on chairs in the West Midlands, the north west (i.e. Cheshire and Lancashire), and the East Midlands, stretching from Lincolnshire up to Northumberland. It is a strong straight-grained timber that can be steam bent easily for back posts, and slats etc. The best ash is fairly quick growing with 8–10 rings per 25mm (1in). Ash was also used for Windsor chair seats as an alternative to elm, and for Windsor chair hoop-backs and armrests.

Alder

Alder likes to grow in damp areas near ponds and streams, for example the shores of Loch Lomond. It is a reddish-brown colour and can be simulated to have an appearance similar to mahogany. It is used to a small extent on ladderback chairs in the north west of England, and is also seen in Scottish chairs. It turns well but tends to be in short supply compared with other woods.

Beech, Elm, Yew and Walnut

These four woods were those traditionally used for Windsor chairs of the Thames Valley. For example, on Windsor chairs c. 1760 from the Chilterns, the timbers typically used were elm for the seat board, beech for the legs, cherry for the stick back, and walnut for the armrest.

Elm, which is sadly in short supply due to Dutch Elm disease, is an ideal seatboard material because of its convoluted nature, which makes it very resistant against cracking. It has a warm brown coloration and there is probably no better seat material if you can get it. It was also used for chair-spindle work in different regions of England, and for joined hollow-seat chairs from East Anglia. There are small pockets of elm still surviving in parts of Britain.

Beech is a pale close-grained wood with a small fleck and is slightly stronger than oak. It turns up in chairs from almost any region of England, though more predominantly in the south. It is used for spindle work and the thicker slats, for example, in square-back Windsor chairs.

Yew has a rich coloration with orange-brown heartwood and a white sapwood. Despite its wavy grain it bends very well when steamed. Windsor chairs made of this timber are a delight to the eye.

Apple and pear

Apple and pear wood are sometimes found on country chairs. They are pale woods though pinkish if kiln-dried with steam and can be readily stained. They both turn well and you can produce spindles with intricate detail without splintering.

Oak

Oak is a strong resilient wood and except on early Tudor period chairs it is not much used for common vernacular seating. When quarter-sawn it has an attractive ray fleck, though this is a plane of weakness in the timber. It is more often used for joined chairs, i.e. those made from square-form timber.

Birch, sycamore and maple

These woods are generally not seen in English vernacular chairs and are mostly used for other purposes. Part of the reason must be because they are pale-coloured timbers and not as attractive as the others described above.

American woods

In America there is a great variety of woods to choose from, but like the British timbers, American varieties of ash and oak were used for chair making. White oak when steamed, for example, can be bent to a very tight radius without cracking. The Americans made much use of paler indigenous timbers, such as birch, maple, hickory and poplar for spindle work. Another popular wood is American cherry. This is a softish timber which turns well, and oxidises to a nut-brown colour over a period of time. This timber, along with maple and birch, was used for making Shaker chairs. Where Windsor seat boards are concerned these are predominantly made of pine, which is largely down to regional availability. Other timbers used to a lesser extent were fruit woods and chestnut. Because they have no depth of colour, chairs made from paler timbers were often given colour-painted finishes, particularly during the first half of the nineteenth century.

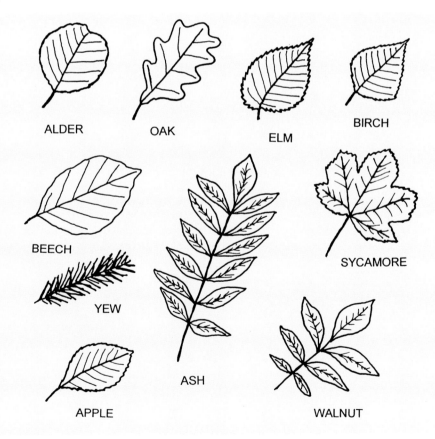

ALDER   OAK   ELM   BIRCH

BEECH   YEW   ASH   SYCAMORE   WALNUT   APPLE

◀ Fig 1.9 Trees used for chair making.

9

CHAPTER TWO
WOODTURNING

For chair making, woodturning primarily involves spindle turning and occasionally faceplate work, perhaps for a stool top. Some of this is repetitive, i.e. you may need to be able to reproduce a number of spindles, rails or chair legs exactly the same. Some parts are long and slender, e.g. chair-back posts, so you need to be able to turn these without problems. Some country chairs have cabriole-style legs so you need to know how to do offset turning.

PLAIN CYLINDRICAL SPINDLE WORK

Woodturning plain cylindrical parts such as posts, rails and stretchers requires a certain knack. Some say that turning good parallel spindles is more difficult than a spindle with beads and coves, but it is really all a matter of practice. I tend to work in sections, say 100–150mm (4–6in) long, turn down the diameter locally near to what is required with a parting tool, gouge out the space between, and then run a skew chisel along end to end. If the cylinder is of any length it pays to have a longer tool rest, or perhaps one spanning two supports; then you do not have to push and shunt this along so much. You may also need a lathe steady for long slender work. It is good practice on work of any length or any that is slender, to finish this in one operation. If you do not, and leave the work overnight, it may deform slightly by the morning due to redistribution of the internal wood stresses. If there is insufficient spare wood left on the diameter you may then have to machine the item again.

BACK POSTS

The problem most frequently encountered in turning chair-back posts, is that their length is often longer than the lathe bed. Most general-purpose woodturning lathes will accommodate, say 600–900mm (24–36in) between centres, which is fine for the

shorter chair spindle work, but not for the long back posts. These vary in length typically between 900 and 1140mm (36 and 45in), and for special chairs occasionally longer. Two simple remedies for this are: first to consider fitting longer bed bars if this is possible, or alternatively to try moving the tailstock onto an adjoining bench. The latter is a system I have used a number of times in difficult situations. As they often say necessity is the mother of invention.

◀ Fig 2.2. Long turned parts.

COPY SPINDLE WORK

Many chairs need spindles of similar profiled shape, e.g. with bead and cove features. An example of this is a set of four Windsor back chair legs with similar triple bead and vase form turnings. Woodturning the first usually takes a little more time than the others, because you have to think where you are going to make the various cuts, which tools you are going to use, and in which order. Machining the next three then becomes very much easier, because the thought process of which cuts to make where has been sorted out in your mind. You also have the first leg to act as a model for the rest. If you need thirty or forty spindles of similar pattern, say for some spindle-back chairs, you will soon become quite familiar with the shapes, and be rhythmically changing back and forth from gouge, to skew, to parting tool etc on a routine basis.

If you have only a few spindles to make, then after roughing the stock to a cylinder, key measurements can be marked with a pencil, and callipers used to check the diameters as the wood is machined. If I have to make more than, say, five spindles all the same, I find it makes sense to mark up a plywood strip with the positions where certain features are to be. If I have to make ten,

◀◀ Fig 2.1
Roughing out a chair stretcher.

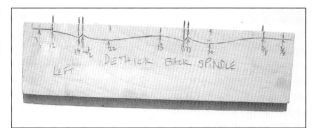

then I usually make up a pin template, as in Fig 2.3, with the edge inset with pins for the positions of principal features. This is offered up to the slowly revolving work to score it, and is both quicker and more accurate than pencil marking. I have a drawer full of pin templates which are used for all sorts of repetitive spindle work.

CABRIOLE LEGS

A cabriole leg is one with a broad knee at the top, narrowing downwards and finishing with a larger pad foot at the floor. Many country chairs use cabriole front legs of simple form, where part of the leg is tapered above a pad foot, and these are made using offset turnery techniques. A plain tapered cabriole leg with a square form top, as found on spindle and slat-back chairs typical of the north west region of England is shown in Fig 2.4. The step-by-step procedure for making one of these, referring to Fig 2.5, is as follows.

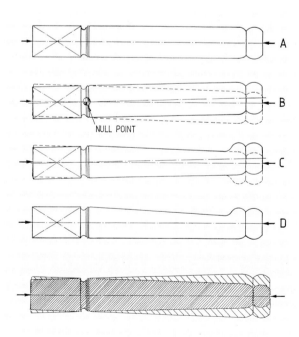

Step-by-step procedure

(i) A chair leg is typically 445mm (17½in) long or thereabouts, so first prepare a piece of planed timber 50mm (2in) square, say about 475mm (18¾in) long, which allows 15mm (⅝in) spare each end for lathe mounting.

(ii) Mount the stock centrally on the lathe ready for machining. Spend a minute or two to set this as accurate, as possible, otherwise the finished turning below the square section may end up slightly concentric to the stock. The method I use is first to mount the square stock lightly between centres, which allows you to nudge the wood over at either end, before driving the centres more firmly into the wood.

(iii) So you know where the square section end is to be, scribe this with crossed pencil marks on all four faces (Fig 2.6). Then turn the leg down to a parallel section 50mm (2in) diameter below the square top (Fig 2.5A). Use a spindle gouge to do this and clean the section up with a skew chisel. Take care at either end of the square section not to break the corners off, which is easily done if the chisel is not sharp. Do not reduce

the ends too much, as this can, if made too small, make it impossible to mount the leg later on offset centres. This is particularly so at the headstock end where the drive prong needs sufficient wood outside of the centre pip to get a grip. Finish the parallel turning by forming the pad foot and the small cove beneath the square section.

◀ Fig 2.6. Marking the square section.

Turning the leg taper

(iv) The next step is to prepare the leg for turning the taper section, for which it has to be set on offset centres as per Fig 2.5B. The waisted end of the taper is typically about 38mm (1½in) diameter requiring the leg to be offset at the bottom end by 6–7mm (¼in). It also has to be offset marginally at the top end by 1–2mm (¹⁄₁₆in), so the null point where the centre of rotation is the same on both axes, is just below the square section. The offset should be towards one of the corners (Fig 2.5), so that when the chair is viewed in plan the toe of the leg is set at 45 degrees outwards, and when seen from the front or side the back edge of the leg is essentially vertical.

◀ Fig 2.7 Turning the parallel section.

(v) Turn the taper section after first setting the lathe speed low enough so the leg cannot not fly out and cause injury, yet fast enough for the tools to cut efficiently. Use a spindle gouge to remove the bulk waste material and a skew to finish. When doing this the centre part of the leg appears more solid, with a shadow effect outside caused by the eccentrically rotating wood (Fig 2.5). This helps you to judge when the taper is nearly complete, and the shadow effect then disappears. The cutting tool also stops juddering and begins to remove wood more smoothly, since the taper has been reduced to a true cylindrical from end to end. Much of the skill in turning the taper is to reduce it such that the gauge just kisses the back of the leg, and the taper is truly cylindrical from end to end. It is helpful to put a pencil mark down the back edge during this operation (Fig 2.8), and when this just disappears you will know the taper is circular.

◀ Fig 2.8. Pencil marking on the back of the leg.

Finishing

(vi) The last stage is to finish sanding the leg, which is done on both the offset and true centres as necessary until the surface is suitably smooth. Work with grits in stages down from 120 to 320 or lower. It is a mistake to try and miss a grade out and jump to a finer one too soon. After removing the leg from the lathe and cleaning off the centres either end, you can if you wish round over the outer corner of the square section. However, it is usually better to leave this operation until after the holes have been drilled for the stretchers.

▶ Fig 2.9.
Finished cabriole
leg.

▶▶ Fig 2.10.
Cabriole leg
variations, used on
country chairs.

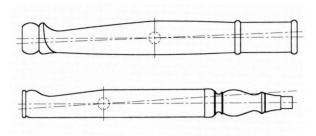

OTHER VERNACULAR STYLE CABRIOLE LEGS

The plain tapered cabriole leg just described is the simplest to make, but there are other variations as shown in Fig 2.10. The first (top) is a cabriole leg as used on north west 'wavy line' ladderback chairs. This is more bulbous in the middle, so when offset to taper the lower part of the leg there has to be approximately equal amounts either end, i.e. the null point is roughly in the middle. The second (bottom) is one used on a West Midlands corner chair, which tapers sharply at the bottom below the level of the lower stretcher. The null point is thus even nearer to the floor, so when rotating off centre the offset at the top is greater than for the wavy line leg and less at the foot.

~ CHAPTER THREE ~
J O I N T I N G   J I G S

Unlike furniture such as tables, cupboards and chests, chairs are subject to a lot of stress because they are sat on by people. So when the parts are fitted together, these have to be sufficiently strong to withstand everyday use and at times abuse. The jointing therefore has to be good, and the parts sufficiently robust to withstand wear and tear so as not to pull apart.

Some chairs use only square section timber, and for these the jointing is principally by square-form mortice and tenons. Sometimes these are haunched (e.g. a chair leg to a seat rail), sometimes the tenons are bare-faced set to one side (e.g. a stretcher connection to a leg), and occasionally a dovetail is fitted so parts cannot pull apart. On a framed chair with turned parts the structure comprises various interconnecting spindles where the dowel form tenons fit into drilled mortice holes, and on a Windsor-style chair with a solid seat board, the legs and chair-back spindles fit tightly in holes drilled into this.

Fig 3.1. Bench drill.

DRILLING HOLES ACCURATELY

For a chair frame to fit together properly the tenon holes must be positioned and drilled accurately at known angles. Drilling these by eye using a hand or power drill is not easy, and the drill tip may wander from the point where the hole is intended to be. Try, for example, drilling a number of holes by eye in line along the length of a turned back post. For chair making I recommend that you use a bench drill for doing this (Fig 3.1), preferably one with a square table rather than a round one, for reasons which will become apparent later. In addition you will need some simple jigs to enable you to drill the holes at precise positions and angles which I shall describe later. With regard to the drills themselves, I recommend a set of saw tooth or Forstner bit drills (Fig 3.2). These are designed to cut good clean holes in wood, which is so necessary if the chair framework is going to fit neatly together. They work well when drilling through round spindle work, and once the bit starts cutting it does not wander.

Fig 3.2. Saw tooth drill set.

HOLE ANGLES

In chair making the mortise holes are by design steeply angled into the part being drilled; for example, a leg hole in a Windsor chair seat might measure 75 degrees from the underside face. To machine this hole using a bench drill, the seat board is placed on the table beneath, which is at 90 degrees to the drill, and this is then tilted 15 degrees to reduce this to 75 degrees (Fig 3.3). In practical terms it is thus better to work from the angle measured from the perpendicular to the seat board face rather than the underside, because this is the small amount by which the table or a jig has to be tilted to drill the hole. This is the convention I have used in the designs in this book.

▶ *Fig 3.3. Hole angle convention.*

▶ *Fig 3.4. Simple slope board.*

▶▶ *Fig 3.5. An improved slope board.*

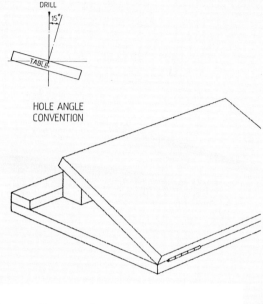

DRILL

15°

TABLE

HOLE ANGLE
CONVENTION

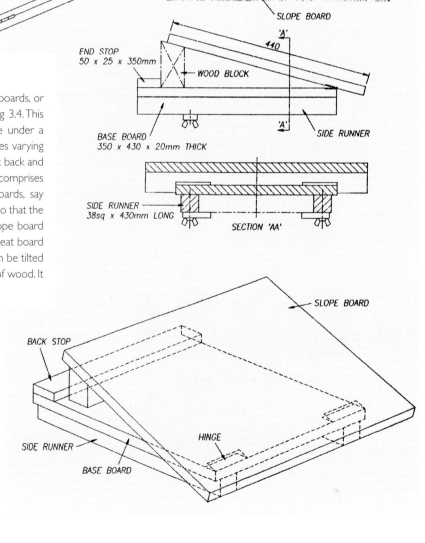

HOLES FOR
BRIDGE BARS

DRILL TABLE
OUTLINE

350

480

HINGE

SLOPE BOARD

END STOP
50 x 25 x 350mm

WOOD BLOCK

'A'

440

BASE BOARD
350 x 430 x 20mm THICK

'A'

SIDE RUNNER

SIDE RUNNER
38sq x 430mm LONG

SECTION 'AA'

SLOPE BOARD

BACK STOP

SIDE RUNNER

BASE BOARD

HINGE

SLOPE BOARD JIG

A simple jig for drilling holes in chair seat boards, or stool tops, is a slope board as shown in Fig 3.4. This device for positioning a seat board secure under a drill press enables you to drill holes at angles varying between 0 and 30 degrees for the legs, stick back and armrest supports. In its most basic form it comprises a pair of 20mm (³/₄in) thick plywood boards, say 500mm (20in) square hinged on one edge so that the top board can be tilted at an angle. The slope board is clamped to the drill press table, and the seat board is then secured onto this. The top board can be tilted to the desired angle and packed with slips of wood. It is however somewhat fiddly to fix to the drill table, and it can also be difficult to clamp the seat board to the slope board especially when the angle is small, because the clamps tend to foul the base board.

An improved slope board which gets round these problems and is especially suited to bench or pillar drills with square tables is shown in Fig 3.5. On this design the base board is much narrower than the tilting section above. This makes it very much easier to clamp the seat board to the slope board. The hinge point is also set in from the bottom edge so that the perimeter of this too can be used as a clamping area. Additionally, two runners 38mm (1½in) square are screwed to the base board, which butt tightly up to the side of the bench drill table, and so enable the jig to slide towards or away from the drill pillar. To hold the slope board to the drill table so it does not fall off, two toggles are fixed to the runners, one either side, which clip underneath the table. These are secured by screw/wing nuts, rather than hexagonal head screws. The reason for this is so you do not have to hunt for the spanner to do these up, but merely need to tighten up the wing nuts by hand. Finally a series of holes is drilled diagonally across the middle – a further provision for fixing small bridge pieces if necessary to clamp the seat board.

The upper tilt board is 440 × 480mm (17½ × 18½in) pivoted inboard on the long side. It is designed specifically so that it will handle both large or small Windsor chair seats, enabling you to clamp one in at least three places without interference, and with provision for a fourth clamp in the form of a bridge bar. It can also be used for securing circular seat tops, though it is less easy to use G-clamps to hold these because of the tilt board size. For these I screw on two 45mm (1¾in) square strips, set at 90 degrees to each other so that a stool top can be placed in between. Thus to drill the hole you simply set the slope board at the required angle, and then rotate the stool top to the position where the hole is to be and drill in. Lastly, should you have a bench drill with a round table; if you screw a 250mm (10in) square board over this, you can then use it as a guide for the slope board jig. To set the slope board angle, wood strips are inserted under the top board of the appropriate section.

Other Uses for the Slope Board

Besides drilling holes in seat boards, the slope board can also be used as an aid for drilling mortise holes in legs, which have a square section. For this it is useful to have a shoulder bar to set the workpiece against, and a piece of softwood 50mm (2in) square

◀ Fig 3.7.
Slope board set for drilling.

screwed on to the slope board somewhere across the middle is ideal. To drill a 90-degree hole in a leg with a square section, first set the slope board flat and, holding the leg against the shoulder bar, align the jig/work under the drill centre, then machine the hole. If you need to drill the holes at a slight angle, simply raise the slope board to the required angle checking this with an angle setter (Fig 3.7). The arrangement does have its limitations, particularly if the leg is long, and an alternative two-way slide/tilt jig, which solves these problems is detailed below. The slope board fitted with the shoulder bar can also be used to chain drill the mortise slots on chairs made from square-section timber.

SLIDING 'V' CRADLE

The sliding 'V' cradle is invaluable for holding spindles and round stock, so that holes may be drilled in these. It is ideal for drilling a series of holes, which are to be in line along the length of a back post or front leg, and also for holes at angles varying to each

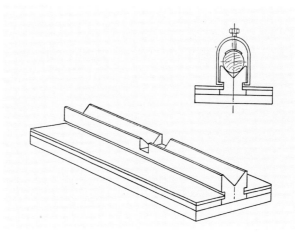

◀◀ Fig 3.6. Drilling a seat board mortice hole.

◀ Fig 3.8. Sliding 'V' cradle.

▶ Fig 3.10.
Using a
square/wedge for
angles greater/less
than 90 degrees.

other. A simple one about 600mm (24in) long can be made from two strips of wood glued together with a 90-degree 'V' form in between. An improved design is shown in Fig 3.8 where the 'V' cradle is fitted to slide within a base board. The baseboard for this is a piece of 20mm (³/₄in) thick blockboard or plywood 180 × 620mm (7 × 24in) long. The 'V' cradle slides on this held in place by narrow strips either side. The 'V' cradle itself should also have a cut-out in the middle on either side. This is to permit holes to be drilled at varying angles as described below. To aid centralising the jig beneath the drill, a 10mm (³/₈in) hole is drilled through the middle of the cradle and the base board. Finally, you need to make yourself a bridge clamp from a piece of steel strip and a small machine screw as shown.

Using the 'V' cradle

Set the 'V' jig on the drill table with the cradle removed. Screw a short piece of 10mm (³/₈in) steel bar in the drill chuck and feed this through the hole in the base board to align the cradle centrally under the drill press. Clamp the board firmly to the drill table, then slide in the 'V' cradle. The jig is now ready for use and cylindrical parts can be placed in the 'V' groove and held tightly against turning using the bridge clamp. Protect the workpiece against bruising by sandwiching a small piece of steel/leather under the screw end.

To drill a series of holes in line, simply slide the cradle and workpiece along under the drill to the required positions, and then machine each hole. To drill a pair of holes at 90 degrees to each other, first drill one hole, then release the spindle and move this along to the middle gap and turn this through 90 degrees. Insert a tightly fitting dowel in the first hole, and use an angle setter to set the angle to 90 degrees. Alternatively, use a small square set against

▶ Fig 3.9 Using
an angle setter
with the "V" cradle.

this and the edge of the drill to check the angle. When set, clamp the workpiece, and slide the 'V' cradle along to the position where a 90-degree hole is required and drill in. If you want to drill a hole a few degrees more or less than 90 degrees, as would be needed for the stretchers of a chair where the front legs are set wider than the back posts, again you can use the angle setter to check this (Fig 3.9). Alternatively, make a small wood wedge and use this coupled with a square to set the angle (Fig 3.10).

TWO WAY SLIDE/TILT JIG

While the 'V' cradle just described is ideal for drilling holes in round stock, when you need to drill holes in legs and corner posts where part of these are of square section, other solutions have to be used. As mentioned above the slope board could be used for drilling these mortise holes, but there are limitations on the leg length which can be handled. Further difficulties arise in the case of back posts, because these are often steam bent at seat level, and this makes clamping for drilling more troublesome, particularly when they need to be secured with the bent side down. A jig that I developed to

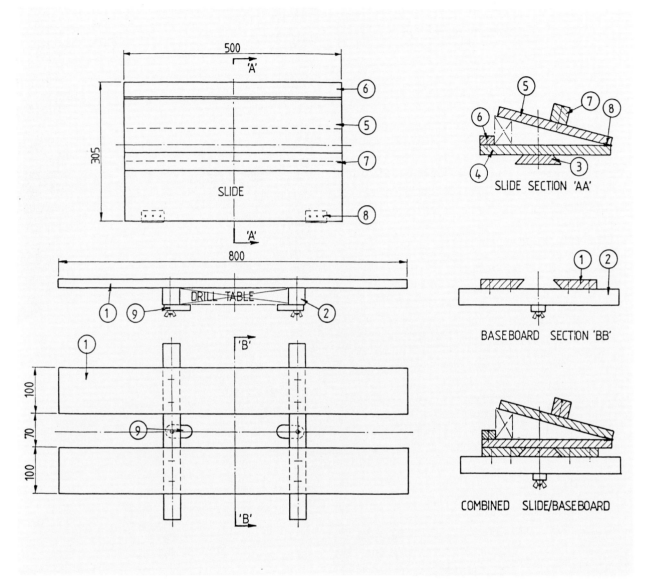

overcome this is the two-way slide/tilt jig (Fig 3.11). In principle it is a jig which can slide in two directions towards the pillar and transversely, and carries a tilt board which can angled up to, say, 15 degrees. The design is such that the two side boards, which carry the slide leave a space/trough in the middle at either end of the slide. Thus the square section of a back post can be clamped to the slide tilt board with the bent section overhanging down into the gap.

Construction

This is made out of 20mm (³/₄in) plywood and softwood, and borrows ideas from the slope board and the 'V' cradle.

The base consists of two long boards (1) screwed to a pair of side bearers (2) with a gap of about 70mm (2³/₄in) in between. Fitted over this is a slideboard (4) glued to a dovetail runner (3), the latter sliding between the mitred edges of the long boards (1). The jig sits on the square drill press table similar to the slope board, with the runners beneath butting up to the edges. This enables the jig to move towards/away from the pillar of the drill stand. Twist clips and screw/wingnut fixtures (9) are used underneath as for the slope board, to clamp the jig to the drill table. On top of the slide board (4) is hinged a tilt board.

TWO-WAY SLIDE/TILT JIG COMPONENTS

Item	Description	No	Material	Dimensions
1	Long board	2	Plywood	100 × 20 × 800mm
				94 × ³⁄₄ × 31 ¹⁄₂in long
2	Side bearer	2	Softwood	38mm sq × 380mm long
				1¹⁄₂in sq × 15in long
3	Dovetail runner	1	Plywood	100 × 12 × 500mm long
				4 × ¹⁄₂ × 19³⁄₄in long
4	Slide board	1	Plywood	305 × 20 × 500mm long
				(12 × ³⁄₄ × 19³⁄₄ in long)
5	Tilt board	1	Plywood	270 × 20 × 500mm long
				10⁵⁄₈ × ³⁄₄ × 19³⁄₄in long
6	Back strip	1	Plywood	32 × 20 × 500mm long
				1¹⁄₄ × ³⁄₄ × 19³⁄₄in long
7	Shoulder bar	1	Softwood	45mm sq × 500 mm long
				1³⁄₄in sq × 19³⁄₄in long
8	Hinge	2	Steel	75 × 25mm long
				3 × 1in long
9	Twist cap/screw/ wingnut	4	Wood/steel	Make from scrap material

Using two way slide/tilt jig

The two-way slide/tilt jig is very easy to use. Having secured it to the drill table, you then place the back post against the shoulder bar, and manoeuvre the jig about until it is aligned correctly under the drill centre, so you can machine the hole. This jig is suitable for chain drilling mortise slots as might be needed for chairs made of square section wood (e.g. East Anglia hollow-seat chair), and similarly for cutting the slots for chair backs fitted with slats.

LEG END TRIMMER

One other jig which I have found useful is a leg end trimmer is designed for use with a bandsaw mitre guide. Attached to the mitre guide is an adjustable fence which has a 'T' groove on the front face secured with wingnut fixtures. In front of this is a leg carrier which is clamped to the adjustable fence using small flat-ended G-clamps. At either end of the leg carrier are two screw-fixed wood stops, which are drilled with holes to fit the ends of the leg being trimmed. The stop at the bandsaw blade end is adjustable in a small slot cut in the end of the leg carrier, so that the leg can be clamped tightly prior to being trimmed. The details depend to some extent on the bandsaw being used, and the jig is better suited to those with a reasonable sized table. A simpler leg end trimmer is shown in Fig 3.13.

▼ *Fig 3.12 Using the two-way slide/tilt jig.*

JIGS FOR LATHES

For those of you with a woodturning lathe but without a bench drill the suggestions above for simple jigs may seem of limited use. However, with a little thought it is quite possible to devise alternative jigs based on the above ideas, which you can mount on the lathe. The headstock spindle can be fitted with a drill chuck, and the tailstock with a suitable jig can be used as a means to push the leg or spindle towards the headstock, thus drilling the hole. It is generally much easier to devise jigs for woodturning lathes which have two bed bars rather than one, and the designs are left to the reader. Some idea of what can be done with a little ingenuity is shown in Fig 3.14.

◄ Fig 3.14 Lathe drilling jig.

CHAPTER FOUR
STEAM BENDING

Many people are put off by steam bending of wood, but for chair making you really do need to learn this skill sooner or later. You could decide to make only chairs which do not have the need for this technique; however this puts limitations on the range of chair types you can build. It can also affect the comfort of those which you could make without using steam bending, but which would benefit from using this skill. For example the comfort of a spindle or ladder-back chair where the back posts have been bent, is much superior to one where these are left straight.

The parts of chairs which might need to be steam bent include slats, back posts, round-section spindle work, Windsor chair hoop-backs, armrests and crinoline stretchers. Bending chair slats and back posts is relatively easy, bending spindles needs a little more skill and bending Windsor backs requires a slightly more sophisticated technique. Let's look first at the principles of steam bending, and then consider the practical application for chair making.

PRINCIPLES OF STEAM BENDING
Many woodworkers I know see steam bending as difficult, and a barrier to progress in this direction. But it need not be, and it really is quite simple when you get to know the basic method. For success you need to understand the principles of steam bending, the importance of selecting the right wood and its ideal moisture conditions, and to know what part of a plank is the best to choose. Armed with this knowledge and a few other useful tips, you can then make a steamer together with simple moulds and jigs, which will enable you to bend wood to the curve you need.

Air-dried wood is normally a stiff material, but if you heat it in a steam atmosphere, you can soften the fibres so that they become semi-plastic and can be deformed. In this condition the wood can be made to bend under controlled conditions, and later after it cools and dries out, it will regain its stiffness and retain its new deformed shape. Typically wood which is 25mm (1in) thick needs an hour's steaming before it can be made to bend.

Tension and compression
The perennial problem in bending a piece of wood is to prevent it from cracking. When you deform timber, stresses are induced in it, and the fibres on the outside will be subject to tension, and those on the inside will be compressed (Fig 4.1). Wood that is in tension cannot be stretched much without the fibres breaking, even when aided by the process of steaming. Fibres that are compressed, however, have an ability to crush or wrinkle together, and later when the wood dries out, these regain much of their strength and hardness. Typically wood will exhibit symptoms of tension failure if stretched much more than 2%, but can often be compressed by as much as 30% without significant problems.

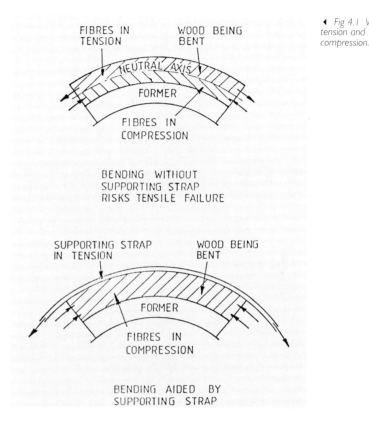

◀ Fig 4.1 Wood tension and compression.

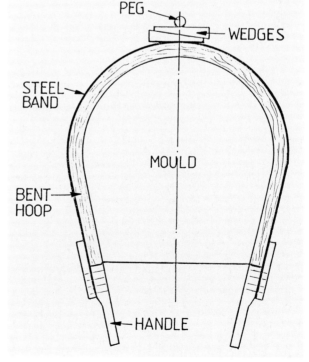

◀ Fig 4.2 Set-up for bending a Windsor chair back.

▶ Fig 4.3
Choosing the
straight timber
from the edge of
the tree.

For timber that has only a shallow curve, e.g. slats and chair back posts, you can usually steam these and bend them under a simple press, and tension failure will not occur. For thicker sections of significant curvature, such as the hoop back for a Windsor chair, steaming by itself is not sufficient to prevent tension failure on the outside of a bend. So for these and other similar situations we have to devise a means of placing the fibres almost totally into compression. For a Windsor chair back this is done with the aid of a flexible metal strap fitted as shown in Fig 4.2. This strap has handles at either end to enable you to pull the bend round the former, and end stops are fitted to apply compressive pressure to the ends of the timber strip as the bend is worked. Thus the metal strap is put in tension and the wood strip inside is held compressed. For the designs in this book wood bending aided with a metal strap is mostly not necessary, though there are one or two cases where you do need to use one to prevent tension failure.

Wood species

The choice of wood for bending is very important. Some are relatively easy to bend while others are extremely difficult to deform. Table 1 gives the bending properties of a number of common European and North American hardwoods. These temperate timbers are ideal for making country chairs and indeed are a primary choice. Two other chair-making timbers, American cherry and maple, are also suitable for bending. Listed for comparison are two tropical woods, mahogany and teak, which are much more difficult to deform and so not used. Coniferous timbers will also not bend easily.

TABLE 1: WOOD BENDING PROPERTIES

Wood	Maximum bending radius for 25mm/1in-thick timber	
	Unsupported	Supported
European		
Ash	300mm/12 in	64mm/2½in
Beech	330mm/13 in	38mm/1½in
Cherry (fruiting)	430mm/17in	50mm/2in
Elm (English)	340mm/13½in	38mm/1½in
Oak	330mm/13in	50mm/2in
Yew	420mm/16½in	220mm/8½in
North American		
Ash	330mm/13in	115mm/4½in
Birch (Canadian)	300mm/12in	75mm/3in
Hickory	380mm/15in	45mm/1¾in
Oak (White)	330mm/13in	13mm/½in
Tropical		
Mahogany	910mm/36in	840mm/33in
Teak	890mm/35in	460mm/18in

Source: *Woodbending Handbook*, Forest Products Research Laboratory

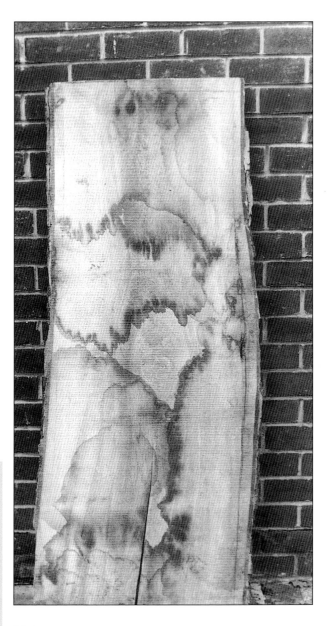

Moisture content

Much has been said about the ideal moisture content of the wood to be bent. Freshly felled green timber can be bent successfully though stresses can build up internally due to the sap trapped in the cells which can cause the wood to rupture. Conversely kiln-dried wood is generally too dry, certainly for anything thicker than a slat and should not be used. Air-dried wood is generally acceptable, but not for some types of bend, and wood which has been only partially air-dried is usually considered ideal. The best condition is one where the wood has dried so it has lost the 'free water' contained in the cell cavities, and the

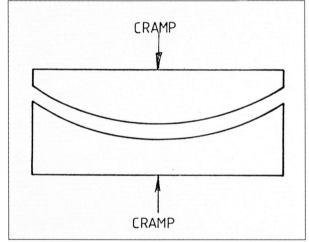

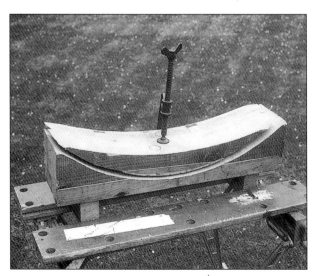

'bound water' in the cell walls has only just started to dry. At this point the space between the cells is filled with air, and the cell walls are still damp and pliable, making the wood easier to be compressed and bent. The bound water content dictated by the relative humidity is typically, say, 30% for 100% humidity, but as the wood air-dries, it reduces to an equilibrium moisture content of perhaps 18–20% when the humidity is, say, 80%.

Wood grain

Having chosen the wood species you need to consider the plank itself, from which you plan to cut the piece of timber to be bent. Ideally you are looking for wood with the straightest grain possible and timber towards the outside of the tree is thus preferred (Fig 4.3). Timber with a convoluted grain, or that is near the pith, should be avoided. It is very important that the wood is free from any knots and shakes (even small ones), as apart from the local weakness these cause, the bend will deform unpredictably in these areas. So when you are at the saw mill spend a little time selecting the plank, and quiz the mill owner on how long his air-dried wood has been standing. One exception to the rule of using straight-grained timber is yew, where its wildness does not detract from its ability to be bent, but it must still have no knots or shakes.

Steaming bending equipment

To soften wood ready for bending, it is heated in a steam atmosphere for a period of anything between 20 minutes and 2 hours depending on the thickness of the stock. For this you will need a steaming chamber for the wood, which you can continuously feed with steam generated from a suitable source. There are many ways to make these, and the one I use is based on an old Burco boiler adapted to take a wooden lid having a long slot in it, with a steaming chamber set horizontally across the top (Fig 4.4). My steaming box is made from softwood with hinged end flaps, but marine ply is better if available. Water boils off at about 4.5 litres (1 gallon) per hour, and I use a marked dip stick set through a hole in the wooden lid to gauge the water loss. This is important because on one occasion the element became uncovered and the heating element nearly burnt out!

You do not have to use the same system, or necessarily use an electric element to heat the water. A steamer I came across for bending parts for clinker boat hulls, was fired by a burner supplied from a propane gas cylinder, while another used an old hot water tank cut open with an electric heating element. Clearly all methods require appropriate safety considerations regarding the firing source, be it gas, electric or otherwise. A pair of heavy-duty gloves is also required to handle the wood in its high temperature state, and those who wear spectacles need to take care against these steaming up. Remember it is very easy to get scalded from contact with steam so avoid it!

◀ Fig 4.4 Burco boiler steamer.

◀ Fig 4.5 Slat press.

◀ Fig 4.6 Steamed slats under a press.

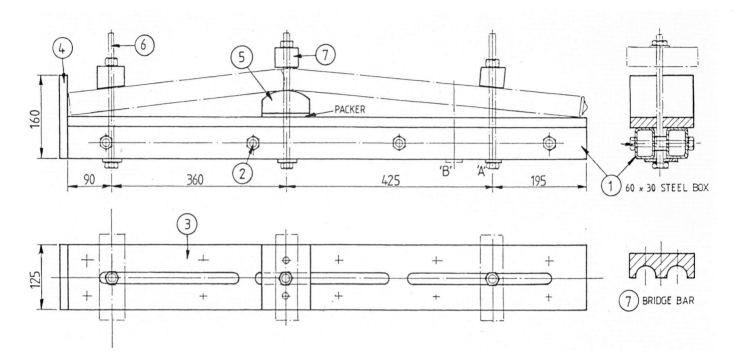

160

90   360   '2'   425   'B' 'A'   195   '1' 60 x 30 STEEL BOX

PACKER

'3'

125

'7' BRIDGE BAR

▲ *Fig 4.7 Back
post bending jig –
dimensions.*

▲ *Fig 4.7 Back
post bending jig –
dimensions.*

Steaming jigs

In order to bend steamed wood to a new shape you need to make a former or jig to aid the deformation. Significant force sometimes has to be exerted to make the wood actually bend so the jigs also need to be sufficiently strong.

Slats

Slats for chair backs are typically 6–8mm ($\frac{1}{4}$–$\frac{5}{16}$in) thick. A simple jig for bending slats consists of two pieces of wood cut with a male/female curve in between as in Fig 4.5. The slats to be bent are first steamed for about 20 minutes, and then clamped as a group between the two mould halves, and allowed to dry and set. Shaping the slats is best done after the slats have been bent. The curvature of the mould needs to be greater than that of the slat to allow for spring back. For a 38mm ($1\frac{1}{2}$in) bend the curvature of the former needs to be about 50mm (2in), allowing for, say, 12mm ($\frac{1}{2}$in) spring back. Make sure the slats are good and hot before bending, but do not over steam them as this tends to make them cockle undesirably. Move swiftly in transferring the slats to the mould, because the material is thin and rapidly loses heat, and these will quickly stiffen up. Finally, there is one design in this book for a scroll-back Windsor chair which has a top rail like a slat, but of thicker section – 12mm ($\frac{1}{2}$in). You can use the same method to bend this, but you will need to steam it for a longer period to make it hot, and the curved former will also need to be sufficiently strong so as not to deform.

*▶▶ Fig 4.8
Bending a back
post.*

Bending chair back posts

To make a rush seated chair more comfortable to sit on the back posts need to be slightly steam bent at the middle. A simple jig for doing this is a strong wood board with a hump piece in the middle, a foot piece at the bottom, and suitable clamps at either end to hold the steamed post braced across the middle. This is somewhat fiddly to use, and you really need a second pair of hands to help you when you are ready to bend the posts.

A jig which I developed for doing this which is more adaptable and easier to use is shown in Fig 4.7. It consists of two short lengths of steel box section (1) held together by four

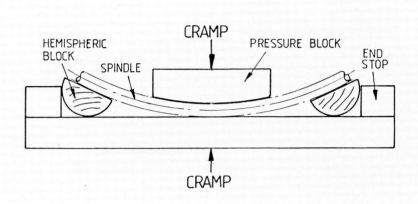

CRAMP

HEMISPHERIC
BLOCK

SPINDLE

PRESSURE BLOCK

END
STOP

CRAMP

◀ Fig 4.9
Slat/spindle
bending jig.

12mm (¹/₂in) screwed rods/nuts separated by thick steel washers (2) in between. On this is mounted a long piece of 20mm (³/₄in) plywood (3) secured by countersunk machine screws, and at the end is fixed a foot piece (4). A loose hump piece (5) is fitted in the middle seating into dowel holes in-board (3). There is provision for the hump piece to be packed up if necessary to give a greater bend, and it can also be moved along slightly should you want to change the position of the bend. Instead of using loose clamps to screw the posts down, three fixed 12mm (¹/₂in) screwed rods with nuts/washers (6), are fitted at the middle and either end. Wood bridge bars (7) are used to brace the pair of chair posts. For legs which are of round section the bridge bars have semi-circular cut-outs, and for legs having a square section below the seat these are flat at this end.

Steaming a back post

My steaming box is made to take up to eight chair legs suitably separated by wood sticks so that the steam is able to circulate freely round these. About 1¹/₂ hours' steaming is required, the essential point being that the chair legs are thoroughly hot right through the timber. You should always bend a pair of legs together, and the jig does not work any other way really. As with slats, work swiftly in taking the back posts from the steamer, place them in position on the jig either side of the three screw rods, and add on the bridge bars, washers and nuts ready to screw down. Clamp first in the middle making sure the bottom ends of the posts butt up to the foot piece (4). Then using a spanner wind down the bridge bars at either end. Check the space between the two back posts is the same top and bottom, by inserting a 20mm (³/₄in) thick softwood strip to gauge this. Leave the jig aside for 24 hours minimum (more if necessary), in a warm environment for the back posts to dry and set.

During steaming the posts will swell by up to 3mm (¹/₈in), so make sure that the semi-circular cut-outs in the bridge bars (7) are large enough, so they do not pinch the chair legs on the sides creating unsightly indentations. Similarly ensure the bridge bars pull down evenly and do not tilt lengthways, else the corners of the arches may cause other marks. My experience is that when the chair legs are dry and set, the spring back is of the order 10–12mm (³/₈–¹/₂in). On odd occasions a pair of chair legs will not set identically to the same degree of bend.

Shorter back posts

The lengths of chair legs vary, some are shorter than others, and on my jig I can adjust the position of the outermost screw clamp inwards to position 'B'. Shorter posts also tend not to need quite so much bend, for which you can either remove packing pieces from under the hump, or insert one under the top end of the posts to limit the screw down.

Bending spindle work

The main application for bent spindle work in chair making is for back rails, and in this book this is needed for the designs for the Windsor bamboo chair, Macclesfield bar-top chair, West Midlands corner chair, and the William Morris chair. Spindle diameters vary between 16–22mm (⁵/₈–⁷/₈in) and so you will need to steam for between ³/₄ and 1 hour. A simple jig for doing this, which will bend both slats and spindles, devised by Mike Abbott, is shown in Fig 4.9. It consists of a strong wood bar with fixed end stops, against which are buffered two loose hemispheric-shaped wood blocks. The spindle to be bent is heated in steam, placed on the jig, and the pressure block is then clamped down. The hemispheric blocks will twist slightly to accommodate the bent spindle shape.

▶ Fig 4.10
Spindle bending
jig.

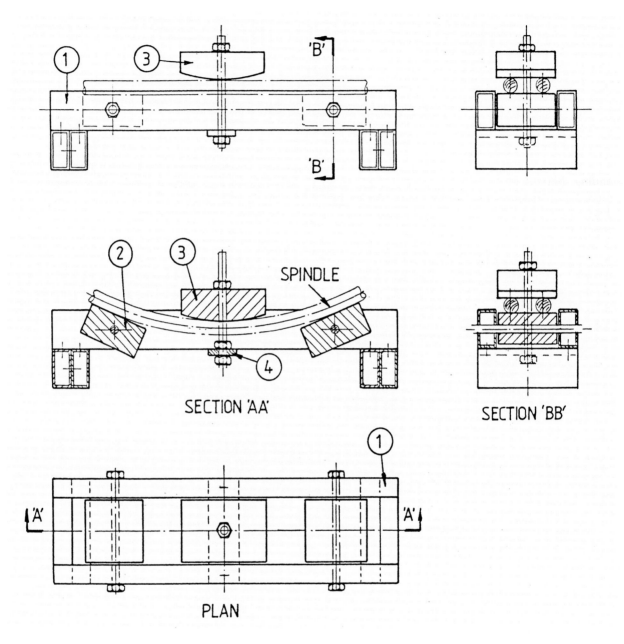

SECTION 'AA'

SECTION 'BB'

PLAN

A more sophisticated jig I devised for handling this type of bend is shown in Fig 4.10. It is built around some bits of 60 × 30mm-box section steelwork (1) I had lying around the workshop. It is somewhat similar to the jig in Fig 4.9 and borrows ideas from the back-post bending jig discussed earlier, in that a fixed screw rod system is used to apply pressure. It is designed to bend a pair of spindles together, which, after heating, are placed on the tilting blocks (2), and the pressure block (3) is then screwed down with a spanner. The jig is flexible in that if need be, the tilting blocks (2) could be repositioned in different holes drilled through the side of the box section, say, for a shorter spindle. The amount of bend is also controllable in that you can place a wood stop over the nut above the cross bar (4). Thus the bent spindle may only be wound down this far. The jig could be modified to accept slats by building a steel bridge across the middle attached to the side box frame work. A screw could be fixed through this and the central one as shown removed.

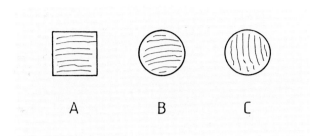

A   B   C

◄ Fig 4.11
Square and round
section timber

Bending difficulties

I mentioned at the beginning of this chapter that spindles were slightly more difficult to bend than slats or back posts. The problem is partly the smaller ratio of the bend radius/section thickness compared to a slat, and also that the timber is of round section rather than square. The latter means that you cannot easily fit a metal supporting strap even if you wanted to. Additionally, because the spindle is crowned over the outside face of the bend, the wood fibres in the middle do not get the support of the adjoining ones as would be the case if the timber was square section (Fig 4.11 (A) and (B)). I have discussed this aspect with many woodworkers. Some say it is advantageous to align the bend so that the annular rings are radial, i.e. in the plane of the bend (C), to minimize the risk of the annular rings parting on the outer surface as in (B), but other authorities suggest the opposite.

Referring to Table 1 this suggests that provided the ratio of the radius/section thickness is greater than about 13, you should be able to pull the bend without the aid of a supporting strap. For the designs in this book the ratios range from 19 for the West Midlands chair to 60 for the Morris chair. Theoretically you ought to bend the spindle work for these without a strap, but in practice I have found that you do need to fit a mini-strap hold the wood in compression to guarantee success for some spindle-bending. Additionally, it is important to ensure (a) that the steamed wood is thoroughly hot right through, and (b) that you act swiftly in moving the spindle from the steamer to the mould, pulling the bend as quickly, as you can, thereby minimizing the opportunity for the wood fibres (especially the outer ones) to cool. If tension failures still occur there are two other remedies. The first is to consider if you can relax the bend curvature slightly, and the second is to accept a slightly smaller spindle diameter.

Cleaning up

Finally, steaming tends to leave a mottled effect on the surface of the wood, so some vigorous sand-papering is needed to remove this.

ᕯ CHAPTER FIVE ᕯ

SEAT WEAVING

On chairs of framed construction the seat is infilled with various woven materials. Various naturally growing vegetable fibres are used for this, such as cane, rush, straw, willow, cord and cotton braid. Cane work, popularised during the reign of King Charles II, gives a springy resilient seat, but is hard on the hands to work. Rush is an excellent seat material, and a well-woven rush-seated chair is a comfort to sit on. In the 1850s chairs with straw-wrapped rush were introduced, probably in the English Chiltern Hills area. On this type of seating, plain rushes are laid alternately against straw dyed blue, green or red, and so the seats have a striped appearance. Seagrass from China is sometimes used as an alternative to rush seating. This is much quicker to work with, because the material, supplied in hanks, is already twisted into a rope. However, the appearance is less attractive and is not authentic. Chairs with rope seats include the primitive Irish Sugan chair, which was traditionally made from straw, hay or rye grass, and the Orkney chair, which has a coiled back made of oat straw. Chairs with willow seating are similar in many ways to basketry.

In America wood splint was used by the early Shakers prior to 1830. For these, coppiced timber such as ash, oak and hickory was split into thin pliable strips. Later the Shaker communities used narrow cotton braiding 16–25mm (⅝–1in) wide, woven on small tape looms. The earlier Shaker chairs used patterned tapes but after 1850 these tended to be a single plain colour. Some Shaker chairs were also caned and rush seated.

RUSH SEATING

There are five designs in this book that use rush seating. The reed used for this is *Scirpus lacustris*, commonly called the bulrush. This is a long tapering reed grown in England in the wetlands of East Anglia and the Thames Valley. It grows to lengths of 1.8–2.75m (6–9ft), with a colour varying between green, fawn or light brown depending on the source. It is not to be confused with the reed mace, which has a brown velvet sausage end at the top. You can also buy rush from Holland and Portugal, but English rush tends to be longer than other varieties, and is said to be stronger. It is usually sold by the 'bolt', but some suppliers sell it by weight. A bolt is sufficient for at least one chair seat and probably two if you are lucky.

Preparation

The rush is delivered dried and has to be prepared for use by making it damp and pliable. A small quantity of the rushes is sprayed with water from a watering can, preferably outside on a lawn. They are left for a few minutes, then any surplus water is shaken off and the rushes are wrapped overnight in a damp cloth or blanket to become soft and pliable. Rushes left damp for too long before use will become sticky to the touch and must be thrown away.

Weaving

To begin weaving, two or more rushes are placed together, butt to tip, and tied to the frame with thin string. These are then twisted together as though you were making a thin piece of rope. The action is one of continuous pulling, stroking and twisting the rushes together, as you weave them around the chair frame in the manner shown in Fig 5.1. If the chair is wider at the front than the back, then the corners have first to be filled in by tying rushes to the side rails. The process of pulling, stroking and twisting the fibres together is an acquired skill. The rush should be twisted so the strands lie neatly coiled around each other. The stroking action flattens the fibres, squeezing out the air and aiding the twisting action, and the rushes must be pulled tight to provide a firm seat. New rushes are added by tying them to the old ones either with a half hitch or reef knot.

As work proceeds, the rush starts to stiffen and dry out. The drying process takes a day or two, during which time the woven strands loosen slightly and can be compacted further together, hence the need to pull them tight as you work. As you progress, waste rush ends are packed within the corner

▼ *Fig 5.1 Rush seating.*

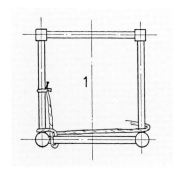 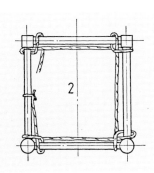 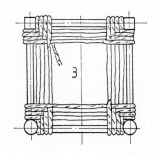 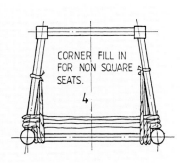

CORNER FILL IN FOR NON SQUARE SEATS.

front and back rails. At each step the rush is allowed to dry so it can be compacted. If you fail to do this, the finished rush seat will be very loose with gaps between the strands.

Weaving a rush seat requires practice and is quite energetic work. I recommend that you first do some quiet reading on the techniques employed (see references in the Bibliography) and, if you feel inclined, go on a course. However, with a little practice you should become quite proficient in a short time.

Tape-woven Seats

There are two designs in this book for Shaker chairs which have tape-woven seats using strong cotton braid 25mm (1in) wide. The tapes are secured with tacks to the seat framework, and simple tabby weaving (i.e. over and under) is used. The method of weaving is discussed in the appropriate chapters. On chairs where the front legs are pitched wider than the back posts the corners are infilled with extra braids tacked on to the side seat rails. You can weave a seat with a braid of different width, but you may have to adjust the pitch between the legs to accommodate this.

Upholstered Seats

There is only one design in this book that uses an upholstered seat form, an American platform rocking chair. This is of a simple form, with plain webbing supporting a cloth seat cover material. Details are covered with the platform rocking chairs.

▲ Fig 5.2 Rush Seating.

gussets, to make the seat firm to sit on. A seat is best worked in stages, first filling in the corners, continuing to wind this round the front and sides until the latter are filled completely, and finally working the middle section back and forth over the

~ CHAPTER SIX ~

GLUES AND FINISHES

You must use the right glue for the job if you are to produce a sturdy, safe chair. And you should not skimp on the final touches, which will give your chair character and charm.

GLUING

Common glues available to the woodworker today are Scotch, Cascamite and PVA. Scotch glue, which needs to be heated in a glue pot prior to application, tends to be used more by restorers, since the wood parts can be separated again if need be. It is a brittle glue, and you need to get the consistency right for maximum adhesion. Cascamite is an extremely strong glue, and where breakage occurs it is often the wood rather than the glue joint which fails. For most of my work I generally use PVA glue, this being the most widely available and commonly used. It is also slightly elastic which makes it more accommodating to slight changes in wood movement.

An important point to remember when applying glue is to limit it to the surfaces being joined and not to let it spread to wood surfaces near the joint which are to be stained. Glue tends to inhibit the stain penetration and thus creates patchy areas. I find Cascamite particularly troublesome in this respect even though it is a water-based glue. PVA glue is much easier to clean off with a damp rag and less susceptible to this problem. It is important also not to make the joints too tight fitting. This is because water-based glues tend to make the wood swell slightly and it can then be quite difficult to pull the frame parts tightly together. Apart from the joints not seating properly, you may end up with a slightly twisted frame which will not stand squarely on all four feet.

FINISHING

The finish to be applied on a chair depends very much on what type it is. In this book there are chairs with natural, stained and polished, and painted finishes. Those which use a natural finish, requiring the surfaces only to be sealed and polished, include the Shaker chairs and the East Anglia hollow-seat armchair and hollow-seat stool. Some designs by their nature need to be stained and would not look right without it, such as the spindle and ladder-back chairs of the north west. Other chairs, such as the Windsor bamboo armchair and the child's slat-back chair, have a painted finish, because this is typically what you would expect to find on an original.

With regard to the finishes themselves; oil-, spirit- and water-based stains are available, with the latter being more transparent than the others, and the sealers generally used are either shellac, ethanol- or cellulose-based. Much polishing work can be done on the lathe prior to assembly using friction polishes, and French polishing by hand can also be utilised where needed. Most chairs do not need a high gloss, and this can be cut back if necessary

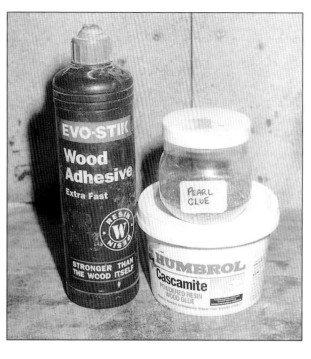

with 0000 grade wire wool. I usually finish chairs off with a vigorous application of wax, which is a mixture of beeswax and pure turpentine. This has the added benefit of inhibiting localised damage which could occur for example if you inadvertently wet the wood surfaces. This might happen accidentally during the rush seating process if you used a hand spray to keep the ends moist during weaving.

It is important to work in a dust-free environment when French polishing, and for this reason you should never normally do it in the immediate workshop area, where lathes, bandsaws or sanders are present. My method of working where a stain is to be applied is to make this incompatible with the final polish. For example if I am using a shellac-based polish, then I will used an oil- or water-based stain. If a spirit-based stain were used you run the risk of the polish redissolving this because they are both alcohol-based. After staining, the surfaces are sealed and then polished. I recommend that you should prefinish all work as far as practicably possible before gluing up.

ASSEMBLING CHAIRS

The assembly of each chair project in this book is given in step-by-step instructions. However it is worth mentioning that wood as a material is easily dented and damaged. So when parts have been planed, turned and sanded ready for assembly and finishing, they should be stored somewhere safe out of harm's way. I find large plastic storage boxes are ideal for all except the longest parts. When you are ready to assemble a chair, make sure your

▶ *Fig 6.2*
Finishing materials.

hands are clean before you start. The workshop is never the cleanest of places, so if you have been oiling something beforehand, wash your hands. When assembling chairs I always place a thick piece of material, or alternatively copious layers of newspaper, on the bench top so that I have a clean soft surface to work on to minimise damage to parts. Sweep the bench clear before laying this as it can be disconcerting to find a small nail, screw, or nut underneath which might damage the parts even through a thick layer of cloth or paper. It is also useful to have a roll of masking tape, especially when assembling chair back frames, to cover the area either side of the mortise slots where slats fit in. This helps to prevent scratch marks on the finished posts during assembly.

One other thing I would stress is to make sure you drill all the holes in the legs in the right place, so make sure, before assembly, that you have got the parts together in the right order. Chair assembly may look very simple, but it is so very easy to drill holes on the wrong side of a leg or at the wrong angle. It is even possible to assemble the chair the wrong way, so think before you do – i.e. glue.

PROJECTS

ROUND-TOP STOOL

As an introduction to using the chair-making skills discussed earlier, I am going to begin with a simple country-style round-top stool typical of the period 1780–1850, but which was made at other times too. Stools like this one were made mostly of elm and ash, but other woods such as oak and fruit woods were also used. It's a sturdy little stool and its appeal is partly due to the beaded-and-vase-turned style of the legs, and also the attractive crossed stretchers, one of which passes through the other. On these old stools the seat tops are more often oval than circular due to wood shrinkage. Sometimes they have shrunk by as much as 12mm (½in) across the grain, so must have been turned in the green and then allowed to air-dry.

On early stools like these, the underside of the seat would often be left rough sawn and not smoothed over with sandpaper. A small

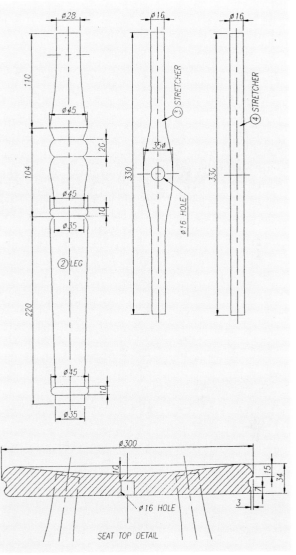

◄◄ 7.1 General arrangment of the stool.

◄ Fig 7.2 Details of the stool parts.

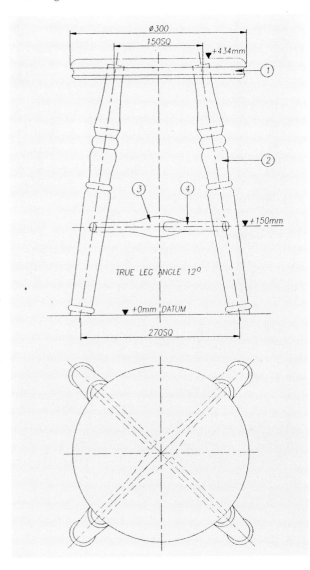

hole about 16mm (⅝in) in diameter is sometimes found bored in the centre underneath, suggesting this was used as a means of mounting the disc on the lathe. It is pure guesswork, but you could imagine that the woodturner maybe had a small faceplate with a centre peg, which socketed into the seat hole. The tailstock could then be run up to hold the seat in place whilst turning. To stop it slipping round there might have been nails or tacks set into the faceplate which gripped the back of the seat. This seems to me quite a plausible explanation, and one that would work very well. Today of course we can do things so much more easily, with all the variety of chucks that are now available. However even without these, provided you have a small faceplate, you can still make a stool top without unsightly screw holes underneath as I will explain.

Legs and Stretchers

1 Prepare stock material for the legs (2) and machine these as shown in Fig 7.2. A useful tip here, which applies generally when making legs which are to fit into wooden seat boards, is to machine these with the socket end located at the tailstock. This way you can periodically test the leg fitting into the seat holes, and still remount it in the lathe. If you work the opposite way round and the drive prong size happens to be larger than the spindle end then you cannot do this. It also helps to minimise the length of spare wood at the end which sockets into the seat. The reason for this is that if you have to saw off a piece to move the leg end further into the seat, this may need further reducing to get it in the hole, but then you will have lost the centre to enable you to do this.

2 Bandsaw the material for the stretchers as per the parts list. Initially machine the fatter stretcher (3) with ends the same diameter as the centre portion. This is so that it will fit it on the 'V' jig (see page 17), so it does not rock whilst the transverse centre hole is drilled (Fig 7.3). When this is done remount it on the lathe and turn the ends down to 16mm (⁵⁄₈ in) in diameter ready for socketting into the legs (Fig 7.4).

Seat Board

3 Prepare the seat material sanded flat on the underside, and screw fix this on the lathe faceplate in the positions where the leg holes will be. If the holes in the faceplate do not match those in the seat, as they most likely will not, then sandwich a piece of plywood in between and use two sets of screws to secure.

4 Machine the seat top with a slight hollow in the centre. Check the underside remains flat, as hollowing wood like this tends to encourage further wood movement and can make the disc bow slightly. If necessary retrue the underside and refinish the seat top.

Assembly

5 Drill the leg holes in the underside of the seat using the slope board jig (see page 16). For a stool of this height the legs are splayed outwards about 12 degrees, so the feet touch the floor a little outside the diameter of the seat top to give a stable construction. Use Forstner or saw tooth bits to give clean cut holes. Drill the stretcher holes in the legs using the 'V' jig, with the drill table tilted by 12 degrees.

6 Dry assemble the stool, easing the stretcher and leg ends where necessary, and then trim the legs so the stool stands level on the floor. To do this scribe these with a marking gauge

▲ *Fig 7.3 Drilling a hole through the stretcher.*

▲ *Fig 7.4 Turned stretcher.*

CONSTRUCTION

The stool here is made of elm but ash is a good alternative. The skills you need to make it apart from finishing are woodturning and fitting together using simple jigs. The general arrangement is given in Fig 7.1 and details of the component parts in Fig 7.2. The order of work is as follows:

mounted on a post, and then bandsaw the ends off using the leg end trimming jig (see page 20). Another useful jig for checking the position of the legs at floor level is to set the stool on a pair of crossed sticks with holes drilled where the leg ends are to be. However, dimensional checks are usually adequate.

7 Stain, seal and finish the parts to your liking as much as possible prior to gluing up. After gluing wipe off any excess PVA glue with a damp rag. When set refinish any areas that need attending to.

Parts List

Item	Description	No	Material	Dimensions
1	Seat	1	Elm	330 x 40 x 330 mm long ($13 \times 1\frac{1}{2} \times 13$in long)
2	Leg	4	Elm	50mm sq x 460mm long (2in sq x 18in long)
3	Stretcher (1)	1	Elm	38mm sq x 350mm long ($1\frac{1}{2}$in sq x $13\frac{3}{4}$in long)
4	Stretcher (2)	1	Elm	19mm sq x 350mm long ($\frac{3}{4}$in sq x $13\frac{3}{4}$in long)

WINDSOR SCROLL-BACK CHAIR

The Windsor chair-making industry in the Chilterns evolved to a large extent to meet the growing need for common seating in the home counties. This forested area of Buckinghamshire and Oxfordshire was once well endowed with ash, beech and elm trees, the timbers which were largely used to make these chairs. It was a natural development then that the High Wycombe area, conveniently nestling in the middle of this region, should eventually become the centre of Windsor chair making in Britain. It is especially known for the development of the hoop-back Windsor chair dating from 1760 to 1900. What is less well appreciated is that while these were produced in the Thames Valley area in vast numbers, they were also made in other regions further afield such as Devon and Cornwall, Lincolnshire, Yorkshire and Northumberland. The Americans also produced Windsor chairs and developed their own regional styles too.

Many people tend to associate the Windsor chair only as one with a hoop back in its varied styles, such as low and high backs, stick backs, comb backs and so on, but they were also made with a square back, as in Fig 8.1. These too were produced in great numbers over a similar period. They are often referred to as 'scroll-back' chairs, the name deriving from the shape of the corner posts which have a scroll pattern at the top end when viewed from the side. Apart from the two styles of back, the leg patterns and turnings were otherwise basically common to both chair types.

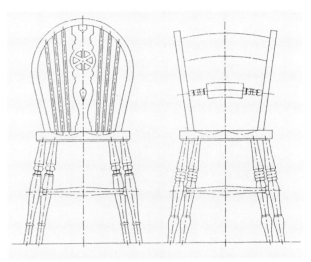

◀ Fig 8.1 Hoop-
and square-back
Windsor chairs.

diamond section in the middle. Offset turnery skills are used to make this part. On more simple chairs the middle rail did not have bead form ends and was similar to the top rail, i.e. it was made from flat-section timber which was usually less wide. With regard to the woods used, the seat board is elm, the legs are of ash and the square back frame is beech. The chair is stamped 'H. J.' on the back edge of the seat board.

LEG PATTERNS

As the Windsor chair evolved so too did the leg patterns change. In the early days these were plain, but as time passed, simple but more elegant patterns were introduced as shown in Fig 8.2. The earliest designs used between 1770 and 1840 were a plain undulating form with a small bead towards the bottom (A). A more decorative pattern with a bead and cove feature above the knee (B) was used as late as 1870. Overlapping these from about 1835 to 1900 was a popular leg style with a triple bead feature (C). A variation on the triple bead leg was one with a vase form at the bottom end (D). Today chair makers still use these attractive patterns which have resolutely stood the test of time.

SCROLL-BACK VARIATIONS

Scroll-back chairs come in two principal variants: the side chair and the armchair. The design here is for a scroll-back armchair (Fig 8.3. The original features an elm seat with triple bead, beech pattern legs, connected by an 'H' form stretcher. Above there is an armrest arrangement with complementary triple bead supports. These are linked to a square pattern Windsor back with scroll-form posts which are joined by two curved rails. The upper rail is of flat-section timber steam-bent to shape, and the middle rail features bead form turnings at either end with a curved

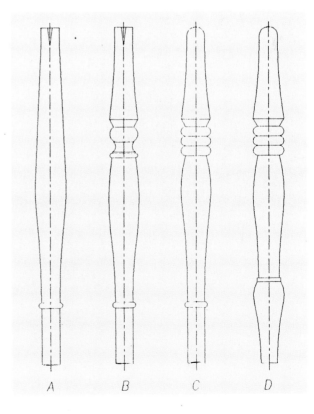

A   B   C   D

◀ Fig 8.2 Leg
patterns.

▶ Fi. 8.3 General
arrangement of
scroll-back chair.

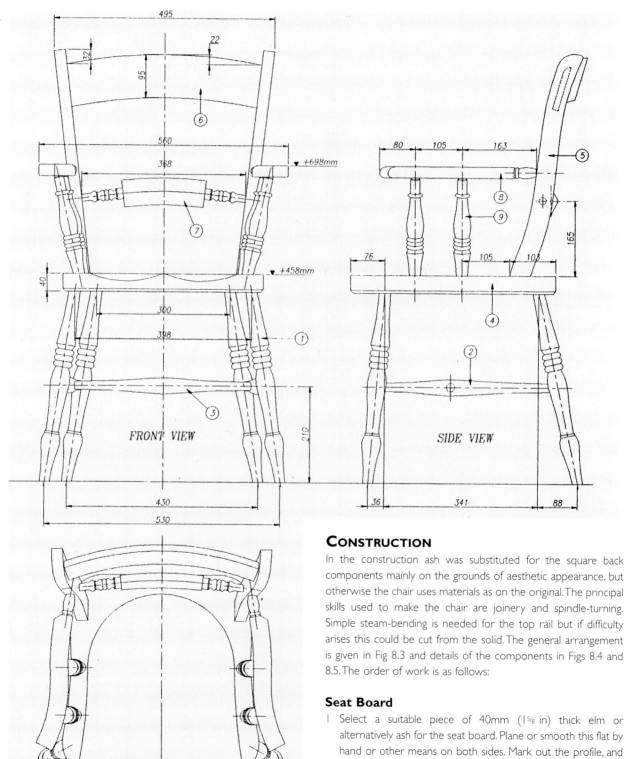

FRONT VIEW

SIDE VIEW

CONSTRUCTION

In the construction ash was substituted for the square back components mainly on the grounds of aesthetic appearance, but otherwise the chair uses materials as on the original. The principal skills used to make the chair are joinery and spindle-turning. Simple steam-bending is needed for the top rail but if difficulty arises this could be cut from the solid. The general arrangement is given in Fig 8.3 and details of the components in Figs 8.4 and 8.5. The order of work is as follows:

Seat Board

1 Select a suitable piece of 40mm (1⅝ in) thick elm or alternatively ash for the seat board. Plane or smooth this flat by hand or other means on both sides. Mark out the profile, and positions of the holes for the legs. armrest supports and scroll back as shown in Fig 8.5. The wood grain is from front to back.

◀ Fig 8.4 Details of scroll-back chair.

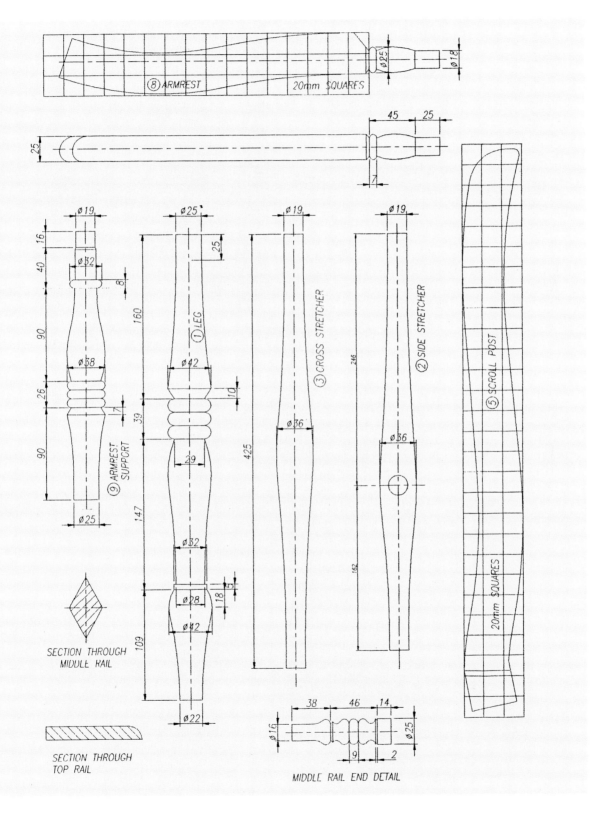

⑧ ARMREST   20mm SQUARES
Ø25   Ø18

25   45   25
7

⑨ ARMREST SUPPORT
Ø19   16   40   Ø32   8   90   Ø58   26   7   90   Ø25

① LEG
Ø25   25   160   Ø42   10   39   29   147   Ø32   5   Ø28   18   Ø42   109   Ø22   425

③ CROSS STRETCHER
Ø19   Ø36

② SIDE STRETCHER
Ø19   246   Ø36   162

⑤ SCROLL POST   20mm SQUARES

SECTION THROUGH MIDDLE RAIL

SECTION THROUGH TOP RAIL

MIDDLE RAIL END DETAIL
38   46   14   Ø16   Ø25   9   2

43

▶ Fig 8.5 Seat board plan.

▶▶ Fi. 8.6 hollowed and back part assembled.

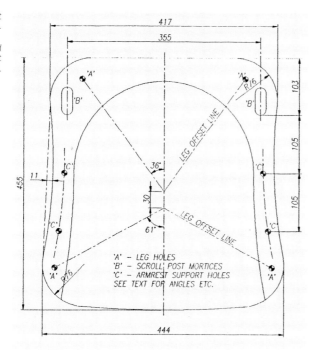

'A' – LEG HOLES
'B' – SCROLL POST MORTICES
'C' – ARMREST SUPPORT HOLES
SEE TEXT FOR ANGLES ETC.

2 Bandsaw the seat board externally to shape, then secure this firmly to a bench to hollow the seat, using whatever method or tools suit you best. The travisher which looks rather like a spokeshave but has a curved cutter, works well and is easy to use (see page 7). When hollowing is complete clean up the surfaces ready for finishing. Chamfer the underside edges of the seat board all round.

Seat Board Holes

3 Use the slope board jig (see page 16) to drill the blind leg holes 'A' with saw tooth bits (refer to Figs 8.3 and 8.5 for the position of these holes). The true leg angles. measured from the perpendicular to the underside of the seat, are for the front 10 degrees, and for the back 15 degrees, offset as shown on Fig 8.7. You can, if you wish, slope the seat downwards slightly 20mm (³/₄in) towards the back to make it more comfortable. If you do this, adjust these angles to 9 degrees and 16 degrees respectively. Use the slope board to drill the holes 'C' for the armrest supports (set 12 degrees outwards), and for cutting the slots 'B' for the scroll post tenon ends (set 7 degrees outwards).

Spindle Work

4 Prepare square section stock for the legs, stretchers and armrest supports. Woodturn these items, according to the measurements given, ready to fit to the seat board.

5 Drill the 19mm (³/₄in) holes for the 'H' frame stretcher using the sliding 'V' jig (see page 17).

Scroll-back Posts

6 Cut the scroll posts from 25mm (1in) thick planed ash. The profile is given on a squared background in Fig 8.4. Use a coping saw or bandsaw to cut away waste material. Clean up the posts and prepare the rounded-form tenon ends to fit the mortise slots 'B' in the seat board.

Top Rail

7 Prepare the top rail (6) from 12mm (¹/₂in) thick ash board, and steam bend this to a shallow curve similar to a slat. Approximately 45 minutes' steaming time is required. A press as for slat bending can be used (see page 25), but should be strong enough to handle the thicker material. Alternatively, you could use the spindle bending jig in modified form to do this. A secure screw jack is needed to deform the rail to its shape. The finished curve is about 38mm (1¹/₂in), so the bend needs to be about 50mm (2in) to allow for spring back. When the wood is dry and set, clean up the rail, shape it to the arch form and round over the top edge as shown in Fig 8.4. Another alternative is to cut the rail from the solid if required, but this is very wasteful of material.

Middle Rail

8 The middle rail (7) is made from a piece of rectangular-section ash, and has a bead turned section either end, and an arched middle part of diamond cross section. Offset turning techniques are used to make it, the rail being curved both in plan and elevation. Fig 8.7 shows the two rotation axes needed to machine the bead ends. As the turning centres needed for this are outside the perimeter of the wood piece being machined, additional larger blocks are fitted on either end to cater for this. The step-by-step machining procedure is as follows.

i   Centre the middle rail on the lathe and turn the ends down to 38mm (1¹⁄₂in) in diameter. Turn a pair of hardwood discs 100mm (4in) in diameter with centre holes to match the ends of the middle rail. Knock these on to the middle rail so they are a very tight fit. Mark pairs of offset centres at either end for the two axes of rotation.

ii Set the rail on rotation axis 1 ready to turn the right end of the middle rail. The lathe speed should be low, i.e. safe enough to accommodate the eccentric rotation, yet adequate for the tools to cut. With your face visor on, machine the end, taking care as the wood size reduces. Keep your hands clear of the gyrating centre section.

iii Reset the rail on rotation axis 2 and turn the left end of the middle rail. Much greater care is needed whilst doing this as the opposite end is weaker because it has been much reduced in diameter. The spindle can become quite springy and it can help to fix a temporary wood stay on the back of the end, which has already been woodturned to stiffen it up.

iv Finish the middle rail by cutting off the two ends, and shape the middle section to an arched/diamond section using a bandsaw and hand tools.

Preliminary Assembly

9 Place the seat board upside-down on the bench, cushioned by suitable protective material. Offer each leg loosely into the seat board holes. Assemble the 'H' frame stretcher, and fit this into the dowel end holes drilled previously in the legs. Gently knock the legs in to bed firmly in the seat board.

10 To fit the top and middle rails (6) and (7) to the scroll posts, first check by measurement the angle for the mortise slots and the tenon holes. The angle for the middle rail end holes is about 6 to 7 degrees towards the back, and that for the top rail end tenon depends on its curvature. Trace the latter on a piece of paper to gauge the angle of the tenon slots into the

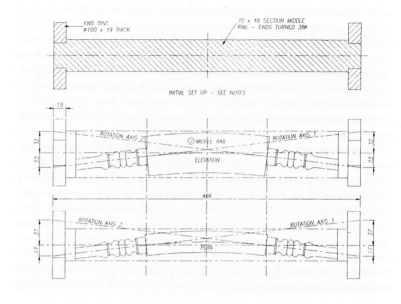

▲ Fig 8.7 Offset turning of middle rail.

◄ Fig. 8.8a Offset turning – initial set-up.

◄ Fig 8.8b Offset turning – preliminary work.

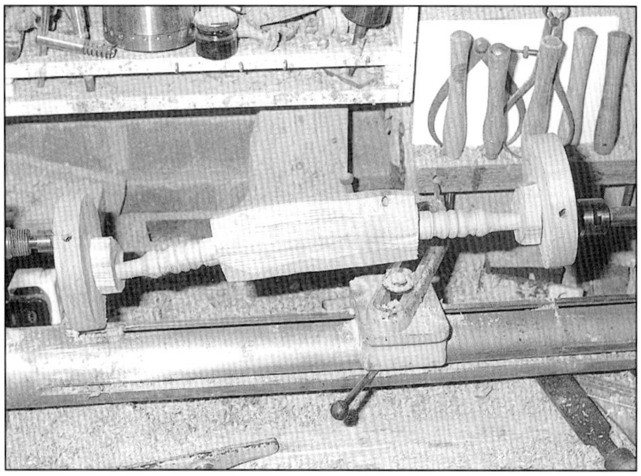

▸ Fig 8.8c Offset turning – the ends machined.

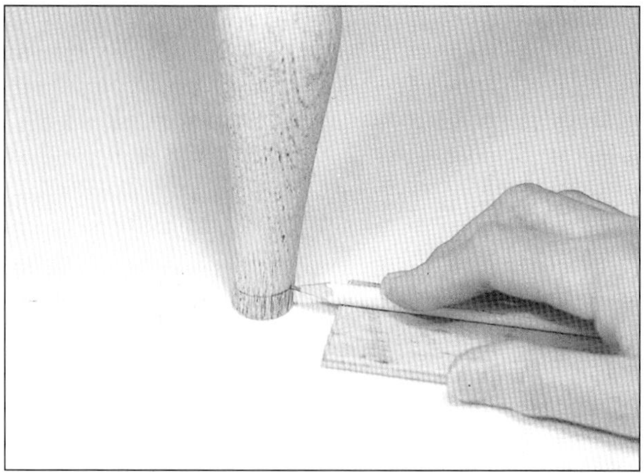

▸▸ Fig 8.10 Levelling the chair leg ends.

corner posts. Use the two-way sliding/tilt jig (see page 18) to machine these under the drill press.

11 Place the armrest supports (9) into the seat board holes 'C', and then offer the chair back together with the armrests, into the seat board mortises 'B', and over the ends of the armrest supports. Do not drive the wedges into the scroll post tenons until later, after prefinishing work has been done.

12 Make sure the parts do not fit together too tightly, otherwise when glue is later applied it may prove too difficult to drive the spindles firmly home. Check the chair stands squarely on the floor. To level the chair leg ends, first mark these with a pencil, and trim them back on the bandsaw using the leg trimming jig (see page 20).

Finishing

13 Dismantle the chair to do as much prefinishing work as possible, staining, sealing and polishing the various parts. A mid-brown stain is ideal.

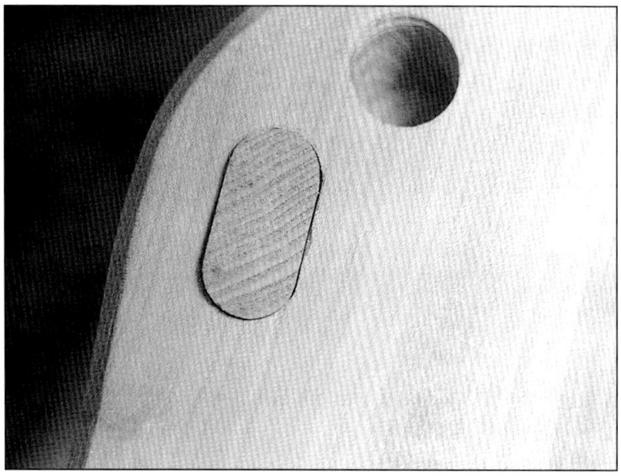

▸ Fig 8.9 Scroll post end tenon ready for wedging.

Glue Assembly

14 Glue the chair together following steps 9 to 12 again, driving in the scroll post tenon wedges as you go. Wipe off any excess glue with a damp cloth. Refinish any surfaces needing treatment and wax the chair all over.

Parts List

Item	Description	No	Material	Dimensions
1	Leg	3	Ash	48mm sq x 480mm long (1 7/8in sq x 19in long)
2	Side stretcher	2	Ash	42mm sq x430mmlong (1 5/8in sq x 17in long)
3	Cross stretcher	1	Ash	42mm sq x 450mm long (1 5/8in sq x 17 3/4 in long)
4	Seat	1	Elm	460mm sq x 40mm thick (18 1/8in sq x 1 5/8 in thick)
5	Scroll post	2	Ash	60 x 25 x 560mm long (2 3/8 x 1 x 22in long)
6	Top rail	1	Ash	125 x 13 x 520mm long (5 x 1/2 x 20 1/2 in long)
7	Middle rail	1	Ash	70 x 48 x 470mm long (2 3/4 x 1 7/8 x 18 1/2 in long
8	Armrest	2	Ash	60 x 25 x 390mm long (2 3/8 x 1 x 15 3/8 in long)
9	Armrest support	4	Ash	45mm sq x 280mm long (1 3/4in sq x 11in long)

WINDSOR BAMBOO ARMCHAIR

The early settlers in North America from Europe brought with them the skills they had learnt in their native countries. Some of them were undoubtedly chair makers from England, familiar perhaps with making English Windsor chairs, who continued this tradition in America. However, faced with a new situation and lifestyle, and a different range of woods, it was to be expected that their Windsor chairs should evolve in a uniquely American way. The turnery, for example, tended to be more bulbous, the seats were distinctively different, and the chair was often painted rather than stained and polished. Such was their variety that they tend to make the English Windsors seem rather restrained, though each has its own special charm. It seems that the early American Windsors were first produced in Philadelphia, but by about 1770 they were also being made in other states such as Massachusetts, Connecticut and Rhode Island, and by 1810 still further afield.

LEG PATTERNS

In the formative years the turnings on many American Windsor chair legs were of a bulbous nature with cove shapes in between. As factory production increased during the nineteenth century, these patterns were simplified and the styles became much plainer. Three examples of chair legs are shown in Fig 9.1. The first (A) is a typical New England pattern, of around 1800, with a bulbous vase turning at the top and a long tapered foot to the floor. The second (B) is a bamboo-style leg that is absolutely American, introduced between 1800 and 1830, and the third (C) shows a plainer leg style of a later date. Compare these with typical English Windsor chair legs, as in Fig 8.2, where the reverse is true; that is, at first these were plain, but as time passed they became more featured though never ornately so.

SEAT BOARDS AND SPINDLE BACKS

The seat boards on American Windsor chairs vary widely; some were traditionally similar to English Windsors (Fig 9.2(A)), but others were quite different. An especially attractive American pattern is the so-called 'saddleback' seat (B), which is waisted across the middle, curving down slightly over the top edges and obliquely chamfered underneath. Another seat style of square form, as in (C), had a rounded front edge and was hollowed flat across the middle. The spindle back patterns also varied and five different styles are shown in Fig 9.3. The simplest is the stick back

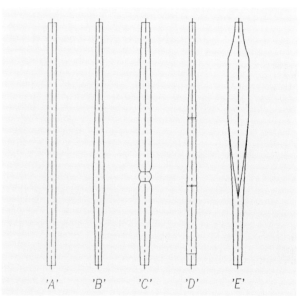

'A'   'B'   'C'   'D'   'E'

◀ Fig. 9.3
American Windsor
spindle patterns.

▼ ◀ Fig 9.1
Three chair legs.

▼ Fig 9.2
American Windsor
seat styles.

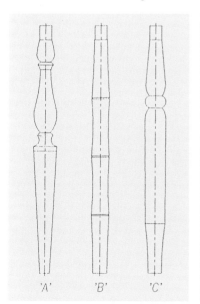

'A'   'B'   'C'

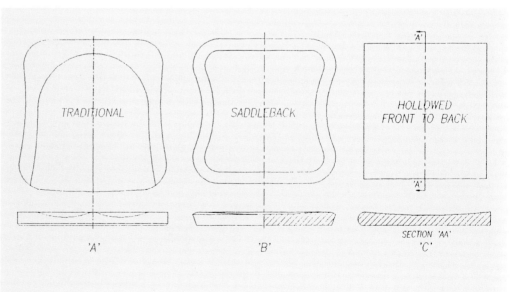

TRADITIONAL   SADDLEBACK   HOLLOWED
                                          FRONT TO BACK

'A'   'B'   SECTION 'AA'
                              'C'

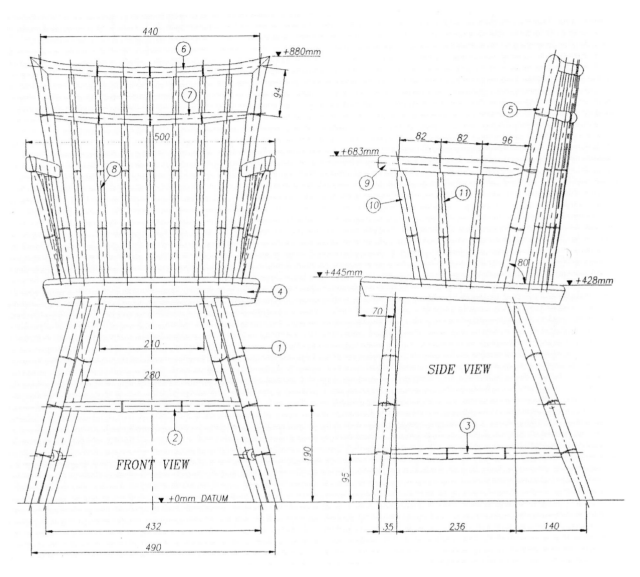

as in (A), and a variant of tapered form with a slight swelling in the middle (B). These are similar to those on English Windsors. Others incorporated a bead form (C), the popular bamboo style (D), and the arrow-back spindle (E) introduced in about 1810.

WOODS AND PAINTED FINISHES

The woods used to make American Windsors were indigenous timbers to the United States, and consequently quite different from those found on an English Windsor. The seat was commonly pine or another softwood, which could be easily shaped and did not warp. For the spindle work, maple, birch, white oak, ash or hickory were used, these being timbers that are strong and could be steam bent. For the slender stick-back spindles there was a

preference for woods that did not splinter, such as hickory or white oak, and for an arrow-back Windsor maple was often used. Because of the variety of woods employed, and the fact that these tended to be paler in colour, such as a pine seat, painted finishes were adopted. Colours commonly used included black, brown, Indian red, dark green, yellow and white.

BAMBOO WINDSOR CHAIR DESIGN

The chair design here is a square-back Windsor, dated 1800–1815 from New England. It was measured from an original in the American Museum in Britain. It was most likely made in Worcester County, in eastern Massachusetts, or southern New Hampshire. The spindle work is of bamboo form and the seat,

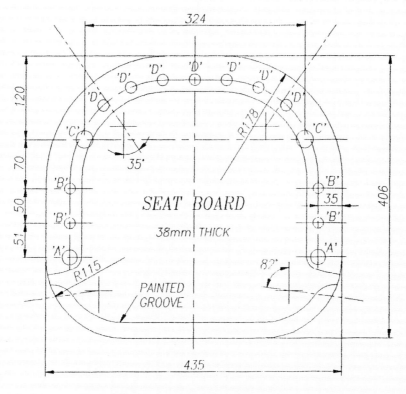

'A' FRONT ARMREST SUPPORT HOLES
'B' MIDDLE ARMREST SUPPORT HOLES
'C' CORNER POST HOLES
'D' STICK BACK HOLES (APPROX ONLY)

TRUE LEG ANGLES MEASURED FROM THE
PERPENDICULAR TO THE SEAT UNDERSIDE
FRONT 15° OFFSET AT 82° FROM CENTRELINE
BACK 27° OFFSET AT 35° FROM CENTRELINE

made of white pine, is similar to a saddleback although it lacks a waisted middle section. The spindle back has double bows, i.e. rails, connecting the corner posts, the top one mitred at either end (an eastern Massachusetts feature). The armrest is of square section and below the seat there is a box form stretcher arrangement, which is a post-1800 style. The chair is painted, and the grooves on the bamboo turnings and seat are picked out in a contrasting red colour.

CONSTRUCTION

The skills you need to make this chair are woodturning, joinery and steam bending for the two back rails. Assuming American woods are being utilised for construction, the suggested timbers are pine for the seat, and maple, white oak, ash or hickory for the spindle work. The general arrangement is given in Fig 9.4, and details of the parts in Figs 9.5 and 9.6. The order of work is as follows.

Spindle Work

1 With the exception of the seat board and the armrests, the chair is constructed from spindle turned items. Refer to Figs 9.5 and 9.6 for details and woodturn these to the measurements given. To create the bamboo effect the spindles are divided into sections, which are very slightly concave, separated by narrow turned grooves in between. The most difficult parts to turn are the slender stick-back spindles (8). If

▶ *Fig 9.5 Spindle back details (1).*

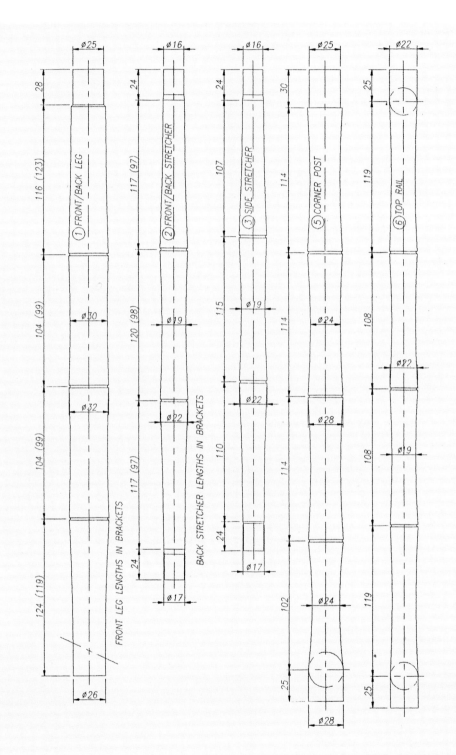

Fig 9.6
Spindle back
details (2).

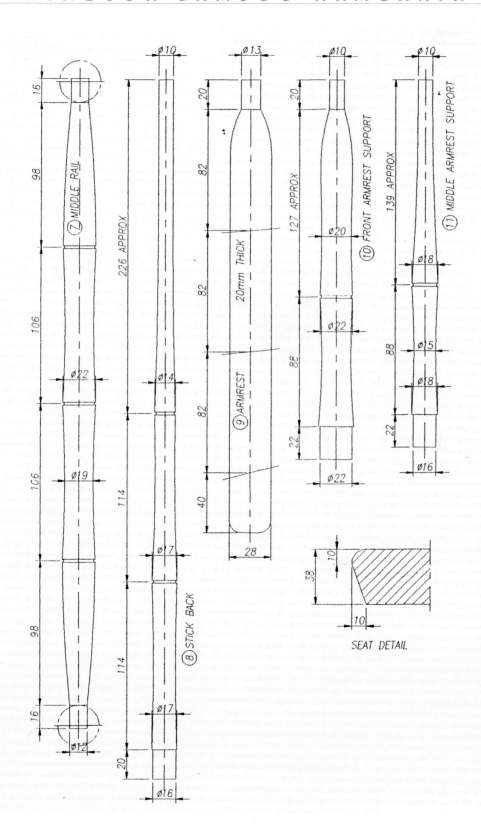

Ø10

16

98   (7) MIDDLE RAIL

106

Ø22

106   Ø19

98

16

Ø12

226 APPROX

Ø10

114

Ø14

Ø17

(8) STICK BACK

114

Ø17

20

Ø16

Ø13

20

82

20mm THICK

82

(9) ARMREST

82

40

28

Ø10

20

127 APPROX

Ø20

Ø22

88

22

(10) FRONT ARMREST SUPPORT

Ø22

Ø10

139 APPROX

Ø18

88   Ø15

Ø18

22

(11) MIDDLE ARMREST SUPPORT

Ø16

10

38

10

SEAT DETAIL

these were plain turned you could use a rounder to make them, but unfortunately this does not create the bamboo effect. They therefore have to be turned in the conventional way, and a lathe steady will be needed to prevent whip.

Armrests

2 Prepare planed stock of suitable section for the armrests. Mount these on the lathe to turn the dowel end, then finish them by hand, rounding over the hand hold end and the edges to finish.

Seat Board

3 Select a suitable piece of pine planed 38mm (1¹/₂in) thick for the seat board. Mark out the external shape, grooving and hole positions for the legs, corner posts and other spindle work as shown in Fig. 9.4. It was difficult to tell the grain direction on the original but in the one made here it is arranged front to back.

4 Cut the seat board to shape externally, then secure this to a bench ready for hollowing out. Unlike an English Windsor, which has two adjoining hollows that merge, this chair is dished evenly across the middle. Use the travisher (see page 7), gouges or whatever cutting tools suit you best to carve out the centre area. Round over the top perimeter edge as indicated,

and carve the 3mm (¹/₈in) inset grooves. Use the bandsaw set to an appropriate angle to cut the oblique chamfer edge round the underside. Clean up all surfaces so that you're ready for painting.

Seat Board Holes

5 Use the slope board jig (see page 16) to drill the holes 'A' to 'E' to fit the legs, chair-back spindle work and armrest supports. The true angles for these are measured from the perpendicular to the top/underside of the seat, and the offset from the centre line. The following approximate figures are given as a guide only, and the angles may vary for the chair you build. Take local check measurements before you commence drilling.

- Front chair leg holes 'E':
  15 degrees, offset 82 degrees towards the front
- Back chair leg holes 'E':
  27 degrees, offset 35 degrees towards the back
- Corner post holes 'C':
  12 degrees, offset 37 degrees towards the back
- Front armrest support 'A':
  18 degrees outwards, offset 47 degrees towards the front
- Middle armrest support 'B':
  11 degrees outwards, offset about 63 degrees towards the front
- Back armrest support 'B':
  7 degrees outwards, offset about 65 degrees towards the back
- Stick back spindle holes 'D':
  9 degrees, angles vary so measure first

Holes for Stretchers and Armrest

6 Use the 'V' jig (see page 17) to drill the holes for the stretchers in the legs. The following approximate true angles are measured perpendicular to the spindle centreline. As for step 5 these are approximate angles only. Take check measurements before drilling.

- Front stretcher hole in front leg – 15 degrees
- Back stretcher hole in back leg – 2 degrees
- Side stretcher hole in front leg – 15 degrees
- Side stretcher hole in back leg – 22 degrees
- Armrest hole in corner post – 10 degrees downwards, offset 18 degrees outwards

Steam bending

7 After turning the top and lower rails (6) and (7), these are steam-bent to a curve of approximately 54mm (2 in). Follow the guidelines in Chapter 4 for bending spindle work. About one hour's steaming is required. To prevent tension failure whilst

◀◀ *Fig 9.8 Assembling the stick back.*

bending the bows, a small steel strap will be needed. You may have to experiment with the curvature of the two bows making the lower one tighter, so the back spindles (8) will pass evenly through these. Refer to step 10 below for assembly notes.

Assembly – Seat Legs and Stretchers

8 Place the seat board upside-down on the bench, cushioned with suitable protective material. Position each leg loosely in its socket, add on the box frame stretcher spindles, then knock the legs in home firmly to tighten up the framework.

9 Invert the chair and check the chair stands squarely on the floor. Level the leg ends using a scribing block to first mark the angle, then remove from the chair to trim these back on the bandsaw using the leg trimming jig (see page 20).

Assembly – Back and Armrests

10 Fitting the chair back together requires some experimentation. Initially fit together the corner posts (5), top rail (6) and long spindles (8), leaving aside the middle rail (7) for the moment. Offer the corner posts loosely into the seat board holes 'C', and then proceed to fit the top rail (6), mitring this carefully at the two corners. Temporarily fit a 3mm (1/8in) steel pin dowel in each corner to hold the top rail roughly in position. Then proceed to fit the three long back spindles (8), drilling holes in the seat board and top rail to suit using the slope board jig to do this.

11 The next step, which is the tricky one, is to fit the middle rail (7). Here you may have to experiment a bit with the curvature of this, steaming and rebending this again if necessary, so that the long spindles will pass through evenly. Having successfully done this you can then fit the intermediate shorter back spindles. Finally, replace the two steel pin dowels with wooden ones fitted down into the corner posts. Do not glue these parts together yet.

12 Fitting the armrests and its supports is relatively straight forward, though you do need to check the hole positions carefully before drilling these. It is best to marry each armrest to its front support (10), and then fill in with the intermediate supports (11). Check the hole angles in the seat and armrest using a cardboard template.

Glue Assembly

13 Dismantle the chair so you can apply glue to the dowel connections, working back through steps 8-12. Wipe off any excess glue with a damp cloth.

Painted Finish

14 Apply an eggshell-painted finish using one of the colours suggested earlier. Pick out the bamboo and seat grooving in a contrasting colour. I painted the chair Indian red with contrasting gold ringlets for the bamboo effect.

Parts List

Item	Description	No	Material	Dimensions
1	Leg	4	Maple	35mm sq x 390mm long (1 3/8in sq x 15 3/8in long)
2	Front/back stretcher	2	Maple	28mm sq x 410mm long (1 1/8 in sq x 16 1/8in long)
3	Side stretcher	2	Maple	28mm sq x 390mm long (1 1/8in sq x 15 3/8in long)
4	Seat board	1	Pine	432 x 38 x 406mm long (17 x 1 1/2 x 16in long)
5	Corner post	2	Maple	35mm sq x 520mm long (1 3/8in sq x 20 1/2 in long)
6	Top rail	1	Maple	28mm sq x 560mm long (1 1/8in sq x 22in long)
7	Lower rail	1	Maple	28mm sq x 560mm long (1 1/8in sq x 22in long)
8	Stick back	7	Maple	25mm sq x 500mm long (1in sq x 19 3/4in long)
9	Armrest	2	Maple	28 x 20 x 310mm long (1 1/8 x 3/4 x 12 1/4in long)
10	Front armrest support	2	Maple	25mm sq x 275mm long (1in sq x 10 3/4in long)
11	Middle armrest support	4	Maple	25mm sq x 260mm long (1in sq x 10 1/4in long)

TWO-ROW SPINDLE-BACK CHAIR

Spindle-back chairs in the north-west tradition have either one, two or three rows of spindles. The earliest had only one row, and the spindle shape and chair framework was quite plain and simple. Later chair makers extended their repertoire and introduced designs with two and three rows of spindles. The turnery of the spindles and front stretcher was also improved to make this more attractive. There were two variants in the style of the back posts as shown in Fig 10.1. In the first the back posts were of square section with a wood turned upper section as in (A). In the second the back posts used joinery skills only, and incorporated a top rail with 'ear piece' ends (B). On 'ear piece'-style chairs the back posts were mostly straight, but some were shaped to a bent profile. Ash was the main timber used to make these chairs, but alder was also used in some instances.

CLASSIC FEATURES

A standard two-row spindle-back chair with rush seat has the following features. The back posts are of square section below seat level with chamfered corners, and above the leg is turned round. The posts may be straight or bent slightly at seat level for a better form. The back splat has three narrow, slightly curved rails, the top one having an arched concave profile with two small apexes. Between these are fitted two rows of five spindles which incorporate vase-form turnings. Two basic spindle patterns were used on early chairs, as shown on Fig 10.2. The first (A) has a short tapered section at the base, above which are two vase-form turnings one above the other. The second (B) is somewhat similar, but has an additional chamfer feature incorporated between the two vase turnings. Within this broad classification the styles were varied, some being quite slender

and others more plumpish. For the front stretcher a number of patterns were used, and three variants are shown in Fig 10.3 – the most common style being that in (A). The front legs are of straight tapered cabriole form with pad feet.

Chair makers also made carvers with armrests to go with their two-row spindle-back side chairs. These were generally taller and larger all round and incorporated three rows of spindles across the back, the middle one of which was shorter. The extension of the front leg above the seat up to the armrest usually incorporated further vase-form turnings of one style or another.

CHAIR DESIGN

The two-row spindle-back chair featured here is measured from an original side chair which is one of a set of six, dated around 1800–1850. It is rush-seated and has two rows of five spindles, with front legs of cabriole form with pad feet. The back posts in the original are straight, but in the one made here the opportunity was taken to bend these slightly to make a more comfortable chair.

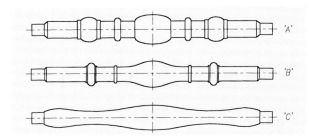

◄ Fig 10.3 North-west region stretcher patterns.

▼ Fig 10.1 Chair back patterns (left).

▼ Fig 10.2 Chair back spindle variants (right).

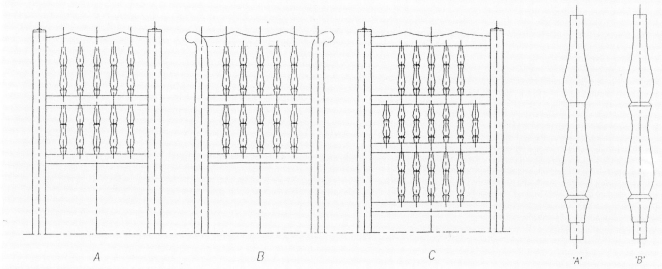
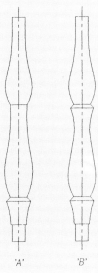

A   B   C   'A'   'B'

▶ Fig 10.4
General
arrangement of
spindle-back chair.

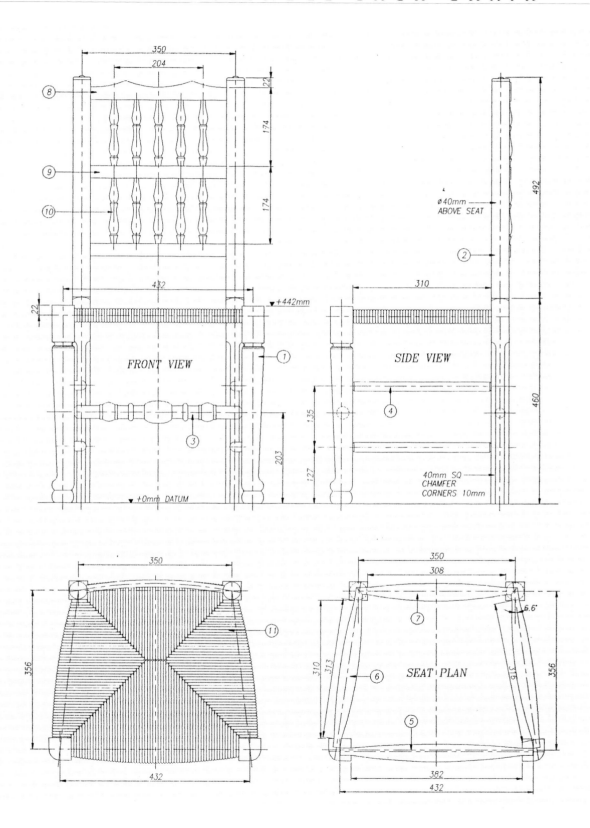

FRONT VIEW

SIDE VIEW

ø40mm
ABOVE SEAT

+442mm

+0mm DATUM

40mm SQ
CHAMFER
CORNERS 10mm

SEAT PLAN

Fig 10.5
Details of spindle-
back chair.

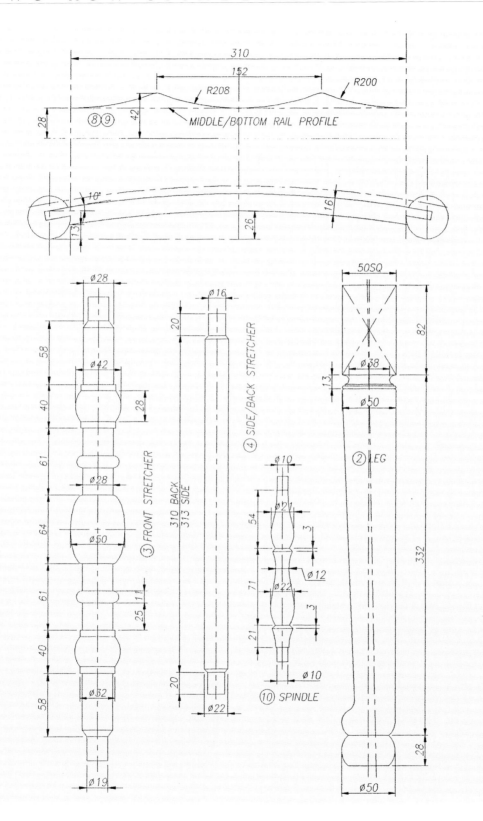

310

152

R208

R200

28

⑧⑨

42

MIDDLE/BOTTOM RAIL PROFILE

10°

13

26

16

Ø28

58

Ø42

40

28

61

Ø28

64

Ø50

③ FRONT STRETCHER

61

11

25

40

58

Ø52

Ø19

Ø16

20

④ SIDE/BACK STRETCHER

310 BACK
313 SIDE

20

Ø22

Ø10

54

Ø21

3

71

Ø22

Ø12

3

21

Ø10

⑩ SPINDLE

50SQ

82

Ø38

13

Ø50

② LEG

332

28

Ø50

CONSTRUCTION

The techniques needed to make this chair are woodturning for the spindle work, some simple steam bending for the back posts, and rush work for the seat. The general arrangement is given in Fig 10.4 and details of the component parts in Fig 10.5. The order of work is as follows:

Back Posts

1 Prepare sawn timber for the back posts (2) and plane these to 40mm (1⁵⁄₈in) square section ready for woodturning.

2 Mount each post in turn on the lathe and centre it accurately ready for machining. Woodturn the posts, taking care at the junction between the round and square sections, and at the foot, not to break out the corners. Use a lathe steady if necessary to minimise vibration of the long timber length whilst machining. When finished, chamfer the corners below seat level as indicated prior to steam bending.

Front Legs

3 Prepare stock planed 50mm (2in) square for the front legs. Follow the step-by-step procedure for turning a cabriole leg as described in Chapter 2 (see page 12). For a straight tapered leg such as this, the offset at the bottom is approximately 7mm (⁹⁄₃₂ in), and at the top about 2mm (¹⁄₁₆ in). The null point where both axes are concentric is just below the top square section.

Stretchers, Spindles and Back Rails

4 Cut square timber for the stretchers (3), (4) and the spindles (10), and machine these items to size. For the spindles it helps to make a plywood pin template, as in Fig 10.6, to assist in making these the same.

5 The back rails (8) and (9) can be made in two ways. They can either be cut from 16mm (⁵⁄₈ in) thick stock and steam bent to shape, or alternatively bandsawn to the curved profile. As the

curvature is not great, there is not much waste material if they are sawn together out of a thick block of timber. I find it easiest to paste a paper pattern on to the wood prior to bandsawing in order to gauge accurately the curved profile. Leave just enough gap for the bandsaw blade to pass between adjacent rails, and put a new blade on the machine for this operation so it cuts straight and does not wander. Clean up the rails either by hand or using a belt sander, then cut the end tenons, which are bare faced set to the back.

Seat Rails

6 Select material for the seat rails, and cut these to the profile given, with turned ends to fit into the front legs and back posts. Chamfer the corners more on the underside than on the top. This makes the outside edge appear visually thinner than it really is, and so more pleasing to the eye after rush seating. You can make the seat rails with a straight edge externally if you prefer, but they look better with a slightly curved profile of about 10–12mm (³⁄₈ –¹⁄₂ in).

Bending Chair Back Posts

7 Choose whether you want to bend the back posts or leave them straight, but bear in mind that the chair will be more comfortable to sit on if this is done. Follow the guidelines outlined in Chapter 4 (see page 26) if you decide to do this. On the post bending jig use a hump piece of about 50mm (2in) to allow for a small amount of spring back when the post has dried and set.

Corner Post Holes and Mortises

8 Use the two-way sliding/tilt jig (see page 18) to drill the 16mm (⁵⁄₈ in) holes in the front legs and back posts for the seat rails and stretchers. The holes for the side seat rails and stretchers are offset approximately 7 degrees. Mark all holes carefully before drilling, and check twice that you have them in the right position and angle, as it is so very easy in a moment of haste to get this wrong. An error like this on a back post can be frustrating,

▶ Fig 10.6 Pin template for back spindle.

▶▶ Fig 10.7 Front frame.

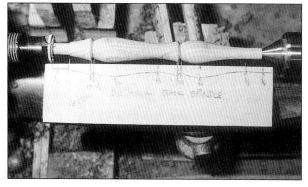

because it means not only that you have to machine a new one, but to steam bend it too. If you do just get the angle wrong but not the position, you can sometimes recover this by plugging the hole and redrilling it. With care you will not be able to tell you got it wrong in the first place.

9   The mortises for the back rails (8) and (9) are set into the corner posts at approximately 10 degrees, offset about 4mm (⁵/₃₂in) towards the back. Chain drill these using the two-way sliding jig again to position the legs under the drill press as under step 8 above. Taper the slat tenons slightly where they enter the mortise, so you can knock them in tightly and butt the curved end of the rails neatly up to the side of the post.

First Assembly

10 Assemble the front and back frames individually, checking these are square and there is no wind. To build up the back frame, first fit together the two-row spindle-back items (8), (9) and (10), drilling 10mm (³/₈ in) holes in the rails to fit the spindle ends. Then join the spindle back together with the seat rail (7) and stretcher (4) to the corner posts (2).

11 Connect the front and back frames together with the side rails and stretchers. Check the seat stands firm on all four feet. Make minor corrections if necessary.

Finishing

12 Dismantle the chair and do as much finishing work as you can – staining, sealing and polishing the various components, except where the parts fit together with dowel connections. A medium brown stain with a warmish look is a good colour to pick.

Final Assembly

13 Glue the individual frames together, and then glue them to each other. Make sure the stretcher ends fit easily but not loosely in their sockets, before applying glue to the latter. PVA glue is a water-based adhesive and makes the wood swell slightly. If the joints are too tight, the swelling can make it difficult to push the stretchers fully home. After gluing together check the chair frame is square. Wipe off any excess glue with a damp cloth. When the glue is set, polish and refinish any parts needing attention.

Rush Seating

14 One bolt of rush should be more than adequate for a chair seat. Refer to Chapter 5 (see page 31) for instructions, or more advanced manuals if necessary. If you prefer a quicker though less authentic result, you can use seagrass. After rush seating, give the chair a final inspection and wax over.

◀ *Fig 10.8 Back frame.*

PARTS LIST

Item	Description	No	Material	Dimensions
1	Front leg	2	Ash	50mm sq × 470mm long (2in sq × 18¹/₂ in long)
2	Back leg	2	Ash	40mm sq × 990mm long (1⁵/₈ in sq × 39in long)
3	Front stretcher	1	Ash	54mm sq × 440mm long (2¹/₈ in sq × 17 in long)
4	Side/back stretcher	5	Ash	28mm sq × 370mm long (1¹/₈ in sq × 14⁵/₈ in long)
5	Front seat rail	1	Ash	40 × 22 × 450mm long (1⁵/₈ × ⁷/₈ × 17³/₄ in long)
6	Side seat rail	2	Ash	40 × 22 × 380mm long (1⁵/₈ × ⁷/₈ × 15in long)
7	Back seat rail	4	Ash	30 × 22 × 380mm long (1¹/₄ × ⁷/₈ × 15in long)
8	Top rail	1	Ash	42 × 32 × 380mm long (1⁵/₈ × 1¹/₄ × 15in long)
9	Middle/bottom rail	2	Ash	28 × 32 × 380mm long (1¹/₈ × 1¹/₄ × 15in long)
10	Spindle	10	Ash	25mm sq × 175mm long (1in sq × 6⁷/₈ in long)
11	Rush seat	1	English rush	1 bolt – enough for two seats

MACCLESFIELD BAR-TOP CHAIR

Chairs where the back posts are connected by a number of horizontal rails are known as 'slat-back' or 'ladder-back' chairs. Slat-back chairs which additionally have a thick curved strip of wood connected across the top of the back posts are referred to as 'bar-top' chairs. In England the bar-top ladder-back chair is primarily associated with the north-west, especially the counties of Cheshire and Lancashire. In the town of Macclesfield in particular, there was a thriving chair-making industry during the nineteenth century where this style of chair was made. Charles Leicester, a chair maker who is recorded as working in the Chestergate area of Macclesfield, and later in Derby Street between 1816 and 1860, is known to have made bar-top ladder-back chairs. His three sons also worked at the Chestergate address. Not unexpectedly chair makers in adjoining counties of Staffordshire and Shropshire also made bar-top ladder-backs. They are also recorded in Lincolnshire, and occasionally you will find them in other parts of Britain. In America the Shaker movement also adopted this feature, and incorporated it in some of their chair designs.

BAR-TOP AND SLAT PATTERNS

The most common form of the bar top is a plain curved rail, as in Fig 11.1(A), or with ends slightly overhanging, as in (B). These were generally cut from the solid. A more sophisticated shape (C) incorporated a steam-bent rail with barrel-form ends fitting onto the end posts. The Leicester family is known to have made barrel-end bar tops. Some authorities suggest that the purpose of fitting a bar-top rail is for a headrest for a cushion or to hang a coat over, but this has not been proven. With regard to the slats, various shapes were used on ladder-back chairs, and Fig 11.2 shows some of the profiles used on chairs in the north-west.

CHAIR DESIGN

The design here is taken from an original bar-top chair made by the Leicester family of chair makers. The original is stamped 'Leicester' on the back posts. The design features cabriole form front legs with pad feet, and back posts which are of square section below seat level, and bent turned tapered form above. The back has three graduated slats and a curved bar-top rail with barrel form ends across the top. The chair is made of ash and is rush seated.

CONSTRUCTION

The general arrangement and details of the chair are given in Figs 11.3 and 11.4. The skills you need to make it are spindle turning, joinery and rush seating. Steam bending is also necessary for the chair back posts, slats and the bar top rail. Details are also given at the end on how the design may be made simply as a slat-back chair without the complication of a bar top.

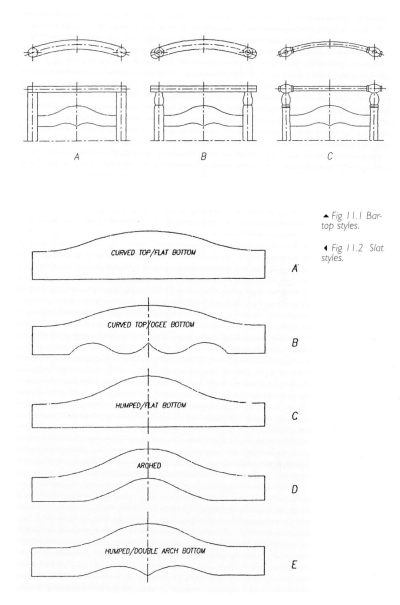

▲ Fig 11.1 Bar-top styles.

◀ Fig 11.2 Slat styles.

Front Legs

1   Prepare timber planed 50mm (2in) square for the front legs. These are of tapered cabriole form, and the method of making them is described in Chapter 2 (see page 12). The bottom offset is approximately 7mm ($^9/_{32}$ in) and the top about 2mm ($^1/_{16}$ in). The null point where both axes are concentric is just below the top square section.

Back Posts

2   Bandsaw stock for the back posts (2) and plane these 42mm ($1^5/_8$ in) square ready for machining.

▶ Fig 11.3
General
arrangement
of chair.

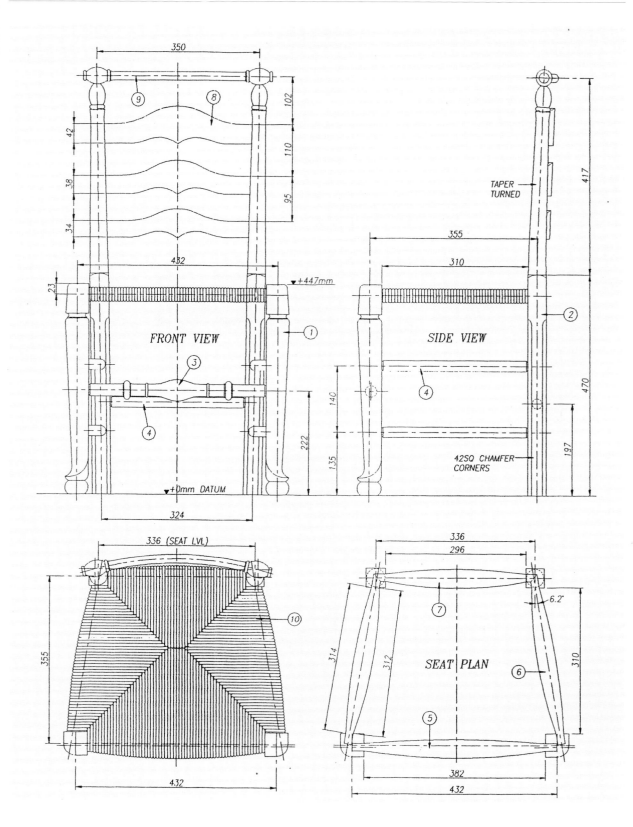

350

102

42

9   8

110

38

95

34

432

23

+447mm

FRONT VIEW

355

310

TAPER
TURNED

417

SIDE VIEW

2

1

3

4

140

470

4

135

42SQ CHAMFER-
CORNERS

197

222

▼ +0mm DATUM

324

336 (SEAT LVL)

336

296

7

6.2°

10

355

314

312

SEAT PLAN

310

6

5

432

382

432

◄ Fig 11.4
Details of chair
parts.

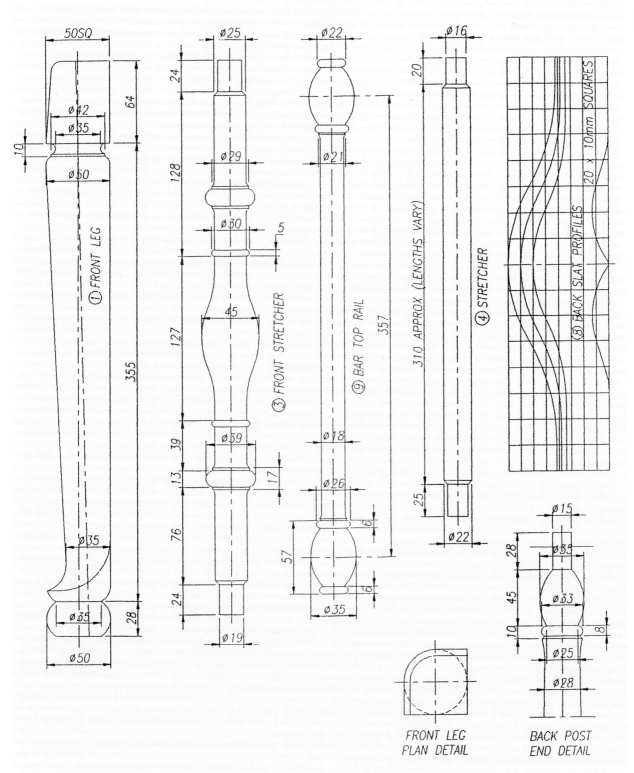

50SQ

ø42
ø35
ø50
10
64

① FRONT LEG

355

ø35

ø55
ø50
28

ø25
24

128

ø29

ø30
5

45

127

ø59
39
13

ø35
17

76

57

24

ø19

③ FRONT STRETCHER

ø22

ø21

357

ø18

ø26
6

6

ø35

⑨ BAR TOP RAIL

ø16
20

310 APPROX (LENGTHS VARY)

25

ø22

④ STRETCHER

20 x 10mm SQUARES

⑧ BACK SLAT PROFILES

ø15
28
ø35

45
ø33

10
8

ø25

ø28

FRONT LEG
PLAN DETAIL

BACK POST
END DETAIL

▸▸ *Fig 11.6
Bending the bar-
top rail.*

3 Woodturn each post on the lathe, ensuring the timber is first accurately centred. Use a lathe steady if necessary to minimise vibration whilst machining. Chamfer the corners of the square section below seat level as indicated.

4 The chair posts are steam bent slightly backwards at seat level, and to do this follow the method described in Chapter 2 (see page 27). The posts are slightly shorter than average so do not need to be bent as much. On the post bending jig I found it best to remove one of the 6mm (¼ in) thick hump block packing pieces to reduce the degree of bend. Alternatively you can place a packing piece on the jig, under the top end of the posts to lessen the bend. Allow for about 10mm (⅜ in) spring back. Because of the shorter post length, you also need to move the top end jacking screw slightly nearer to the hump.

Seat Rails and Stretchers

5 Cut rough-sawn timber for the stretchers and machine these, using the drawings for guidance. These have 16mm (⅝in) dowel ends, but could be increased to 18mm (¹¹⁄₁₆ in) if desired which will make the frame stronger. Forstner bits of this intermediate size are available. For the seat rails, hand cut these to shape, chamfer the corners and machine the dowel ends.

Slats

6 Prepare 6mm (¼in) thick planed material suitable for making the back slats. Steam these for 20 minutes, then bend them under the slat press. Follow the instructions in Chapter 4, and work swiftly whilst placing them in the press. Being thin, the slats cool off rapidly, and quickly loose plasticity. Cut them to shape afterwards using either a coping or fret saw, and sandpaper the surfaces to remove any mottled aberrations caused by steaming.

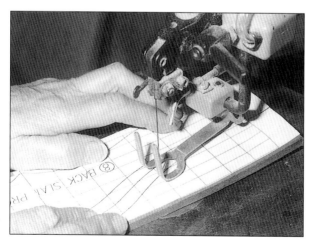

▸ *Fig 11.5
Cutting the slats
to shape.*

Bar-top Rail

7 The bar-top rail needs to be approximately 8mm (⁵⁄₁₆ in) longer than the linear distance between the top of the back posts, to take account of the curvature when bent. This assumes a bend of approximately 32mm (1¼ in). It needs about 45 minutes' steaming. Follow the guidelines outlined in Chapter 4 (see page 27) for bending round section timber. The curvature is not great so it should pull without problems. If a tension failure does occur then the fault could be because the bar is insufficiently steamed, or has cooled off too rapidly before bending. You will have a greater chance of success if you use wood which is only partly seasoned. If you do use air-dried wood, you can lessen the risk of tension failure if you accept a slightly smaller radius of curvature.

Corner Post Holes and Mortises

8 Drill the dowel holes in the front legs and back posts using the two-way sliding/tilt jig, (see page 18). The holes for the side seat rails and stretchers are offset at 6 degrees, and the back posts taper in about 1 degree either side. Mark the hole positions accurately and, to prevent mistakes, check before drilling to ensure these are right.

9 The angle for the slat end mortises into the back posts is approximately 18 degrees set 5mm (³⁄₁₆ in) towards the back, assuming a bend of 32mm (1¼ in), but it is better to trace the edge profile on a piece of paper to gauge this angle. Chain drill the mortise slots for the slat ends under the drill press. Ensure the slat ends fit tightly into the mortises, tapering these locally on the back face if necessary.

First Assembly

10 After all the parts are made and cleaned up, assemble the chair frame together initially without glue.

11 Fit together the front and back frames individually, checking that these are square and there is no wind. Then link the front and back frames together with the side rails and stretchers, and check the chair stands firm and square. Make minor corrections where necessary (Fig 11.7).

Parts List

Item	Description	No	Material	Dimensions
1	Front leg	2	Ash	50mm sq ×480mmlong
				(2in sq × 19in long)
2	Back post	2	Ash	42mm sq × 950mm long
				(1⁵⁄₈in sq × 37¹⁄₂in long)
3	Front stretcher	1	Ash	50mm sq × 450mm long
				(2in sq × 17³⁄₄in long)
4	Side/back stretcher	4	Ash	28mm sq × 400mm long
				(1¹⁄₈in sq × 15³⁄₄in long)
5	Front seat rail	1	Ash	40 × 22 × 450mm long
				(1⁵⁄₈ ×⁷⁄₈ × 17³⁄₄ in long)
6	Side seat rail	2	Ash	40 × 22 × 380mm long
				(1⁵⁄₈ × ⁷⁄₈ × 15in long)
7	Back seat rail	1	Ash	40 × 22 × 370mm long
				(1⁵⁄₈ × ⁷⁄₈ × 14³⁄₄ in long)
8	Slat	3	Ash	80 × 6 × 400mm long
				(3¹⁄₄ ×¹⁄₄ × 15³⁄₄ in long)
9	Bar-top rail	1	Ash	40mm sq × 430mm long
				(1⁵⁄₈in sq × 17¹⁄₄ in long)
10	Rush seat	1	English rush 1 bolt – sufficient for two seats	

Fig 11.7 First assembly.

Fig. 11.8 Five-slat ladder-chair alternative.

Finishing

12 When the assembly fits together satisfactorily, dismantle and prefinish the components, staining, sealing and polishing the various parts as much as possible. Cover the dowel and slat ends with masking tape whilst doing this, to prevent polish spreading on to areas which will be later glued. A warm medium brown stain is suggested.

Final Assembly

13 Reassemble and glue the chair together following steps 10 and 11. Wipe off any excess PVA glue with a damp cloth. Recheck the chair stands firm without wind, and polish any surfaces needing refinishing.

Rush Seat

14 One bolt of rush is more than adequate for a chair seat. Follow the guidelines given in Chapter 5 (see page 31) for doing this. Alternatively, use seagrass to weave the seat. After weaving, give the chair a final inspection and wax over.

ALTERNATIVE SLAT-BACK CHAIR

As an alternative you can, if you wish, make the chair as a slat-back only and dispense with the bar top. To do this the back posts should be replaced with those similar to the spindle-back chair (Fig 10.4), i.e. parallel turned above seat level. The number of slats should also be increased to a minimum of four or perhaps five and made as a graduated set. Fig 11.8 shows a five-slat ladder-back typical of the north west.

WAVY LINE LADDER-BACK CHAIR

The 'wavy line' ladder-back chair has always been an enormously popular form of rush-seated chair. They are so called because of the characteristic wavy-shape slat form of the chair back. They were made in the north-west area of England and produced by chair makers in great numbers between 1780 and 1840. Such was their popularity and enduring form, that the design is still produced today with very little change from the original concept. They were made in various styles including side chairs, armchairs and nursing chairs with slightly lower armrests. They are also found made as rocking chairs. Very few chairs have been discovered with provenanced chair maker's stamps on them.

CLASSIC FEATURES

A wavy line chair back post was traditionally of square section with chamfered corners below the seat, and with a round section above finishing with a domed nipple at the top. Less commonly the back posts were made turned end to end. The posts were often left straight for ease of construction, though some chair makers did incorporate a bend at seat level to make the chairs more comfortable. The front posts were of cabriole leg form, with pad feet, and three basic shapes were used, as shown in Fig 12.1. Characteristically these legs were of slightly bulbous form in the middle narrowing to a neck section above the foot. The pad feet on types (A) and (B) were of beaded form. On legs type (C) the pads were turned parallel with square corners, and at the top on the end face the woodturner sometimes cut incised rings. Research suggests that chairs with front legs type (B) had back posts turned end to end, whilst chairs with the other two cabriole leg styles tended to have posts either straight or bent, with a square section below the seat. On an armchair the front posts usually had a vase form turning below the armrest.

Across the front, the legs were joined with a profiled stretcher, which was typically a double vase form shape mirrored about the centreline. Elsewhere the framework was linked by simple straight stretchers, with two to each side and one at the back. The rush seat was often finished with protective strips around the perimeter edge. Above the seat the chair back posts were fitted with a graduated set of 'wavy line' pattern slats. A side chair usually has five curved slats and an armchair six. An interesting point is that unlike other chairs, the slats on wavy line ladder-backs were fitted in a partially finished state, where the end width was slightly greater than the mortise length. A draw knife was then used to trim the top edge down after fitting. In consequence on old chairs there is a small step adjacent to the post as shown in Fig 12.2.

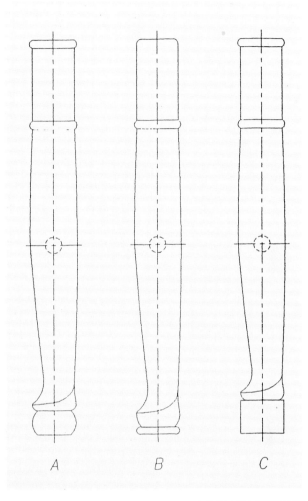

A   B   C

◄ *Fig 12.2 Slat
detail.*

▶ Fig 12.3
General
arrangement of
wavy line chair.

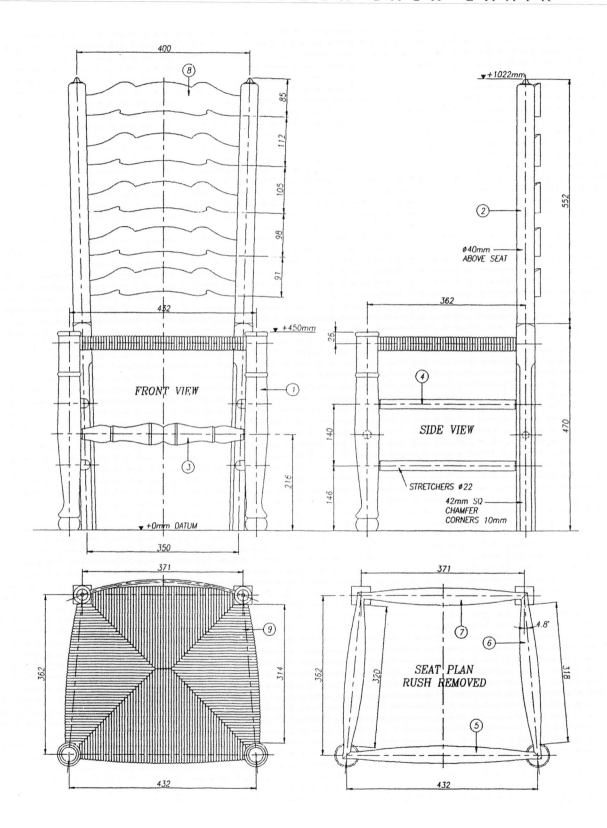

FRONT VIEW

SIDE VIEW

SEAT PLAN
RUSH REMOVED

STRETCHERS ⌀22

42mm SQ
CHAMFER
CORNERS 10mm

⌀40mm
ABOVE SEAT

▼ +1022mm

▼ +450mm

▼ +0mm DATUM

◄ Fig 12.4
Details of chair
components.

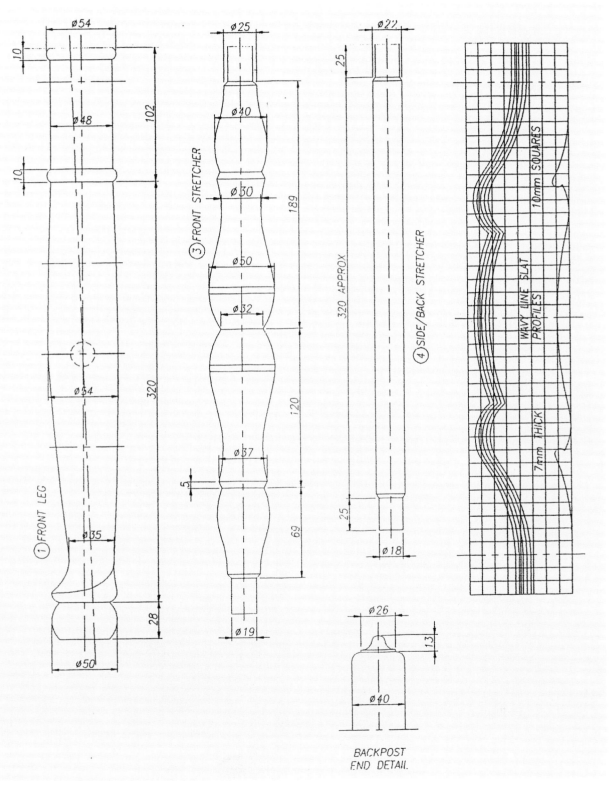

Ø54

10

Ø48

10

102

Ø54

320

① FRONT LEG

Ø35

28

Ø50

③ FRONT STRETCHER

Ø25

Ø40

Ø30

189

Ø50

Ø32

120

Ø37

5

69

Ø19

④ SIDE/BACK STRETCHER

Ø22

25

320 APPROX

25

Ø18

Ø26

13

Ø40

BACKPOST
END DETAIL.

WAVY LINE SLAT
PROFILES

10mm SQUARES

7mm THICK

71

CONSTRUCTION

The wavy line ladder-back chair design here has cabriole legs type (A) joined by a vase form front stretcher, square form back posts with a round section above the seat, and a set of five graduated wavy line pattern slats. The general arrangement is given in Fig 12.3 and details of the parts in Fig 12.4. The techniques needed to make it are woodturning, joinery and rush seating. Steam bending is also needed for making the slats, but is optional for the back posts, depending on whether these are to be bent or not. The wood used for construction is ash. An alternative choice is alder as early chairs were sometimes made of this timber. However, this wood is not so readily available. The suggested order of work is as follows.

Back Posts

1 Prepare planed material 42mm (1⅝in) square ready for machining. Woodturn each post, ensuring the timber is accurately centred on the lathe. Use a lathe steady if necessary to support the long length of timber against undue vibration. Chamfer the corners of the square section below the seat level as shown in the drawing.

2 As an alternative you could make the legs of round section end to end. In this case you only need to prepare bandsawn material, say, 48mm (1⅞in) square, and centring on the lathe is not so critical.

Front Legs

3 Prepare material 57mm (2¼in) square for the two cabriole-style legs. The method of making these is given in Chapter 2 (see page 12). These legs differ from the plain tapered cabriole leg, in that they are of bulbous form in the middle, and taper down only from below the level of the front stretcher. The leg is machined first on its true axis, and then offset approximately 10mm (⅜in) at either end for tapering down. The null point where both axes of rotation are concentric is approximately where the front stretcher connects, i.e. the bulbous point. These legs tend to be undercut slightly at the neck, and the back edge is not straight when viewed from the side, as would be the case with a plain tapered leg (see Fig 10.5).

Seat Rails and Stretchers

4 Cut material for the six stretchers and machine these as shown in the drawing. The front stretcher is profiled to a vase form and has 19mm (¾in) diameter ends. The side and back stretchers are 22mm (⅞in) diameter with 18mm (¹¹⁄₁₆in) dowel ends.

5 Shape the seat rails with chamfered corners and machine the dowel ends. Note that because the seat rails are at the same level with mitred ends, the dowels cannot penetrate full depth into the back posts. In terms of chair strength this is a permanent problem, so to some extent additional reliance is placed on the twin side stretchers and the rush seating to aid holding the frame together. Having said this, there are thousands of chairs made like this in existence that have not fallen apart.

Slats

6 Prepare 8mm (⁵⁄₁₆in) thick planed material of suitable width ready for making the 'wavy line' back slats. Steam these for 20 minutes and then bend them as a pack under the slat press, following the instructions in Chapter 4, and afterwards, when set, cut them to shape. Paste on a paper pattern to use as a guide when removing waste material either with a bandsaw or coping saw. Afterwards clean up the surfaces to remove any aberrations caused by steaming.

Bending Back Posts

7 The back posts can be left straight if desired, but the chair form is more comfortable if these are slightly bent at seat level. Follow the instructions for bending chair back posts in Chapter 4 (see page 26). You should use a full height hump piece, i.e. 50mm (2in) and expect about 10mm (⅜ in) spring back.

▶ *Fig 12.5 Wavy line slat-back being assembled.*

Corner Post Holes and Mortises

8 Use the 'V' jig (see page 17) to drill the holes in the front legs, and the two-way sliding/tilt jig (see page 18) for the holes in the square-form back posts. Alternatively, if you are using straight back posts turned end to end, use the 'V' jig to drill the holes in these. The holes for the side seat rails and stretchers are offset 5 degrees either side. The back posts are also tapered in slightly top to bottom by about 1 to 2 degrees. It is not really critical to drill the back seat rail and stretcher holes in at this small angle, but it does make the dowel ends slide in a little more easily.

9 The angle for the mortise slots for the slats is approximately 14 degrees offset 5mm (³/₁₆in) towards the back, assuming a bend of 32mm (1¹/₄in). As a check, trace the slat edge profile on a piece of paper and measure the angle. Chain drill the mortise slots under the drill press. Ensure the slats fit tightly tapering the ends locally on the back face if necessary.

First Assembly

10 Fit together the front and back frames individually, and check these are square and there is no wind. Then join the front and back frames together with the side seat rails and stretchers, and check the chair stands firm and square to your satisfaction.

Finishing

11 Dismantle the chair to stain, seal and polish the components as far as practicably possible. Tape the dowels and glue connections to minimise the sealer and polish spreading to these areas. A warm medium brown stain is suggested as the finish colour.

Final Assembly

12 Assemble and glue the front and back frames individually and recheck the frames are square without wind. Glue the front and back frames together and check the chair stands firm on all four feet. Wipe off any excess PVA glue and refinish any items that need attention.

Rush Seat

13 Rush seat the chair following the guidelines in Chapter 5 (see page 31). After weaving, give the chair a final inspection and wax over.

◀ Fig 12.6
*Assembled chair
ready for staining
and polishing.*

PARTS LIST

Item	Description	No	Material	Dimensions
1	Front leg	2	Ash	54mm sq × 490mm long (2¹/₈ in sq × 19¹/₄ in long)
2	Back post	2	Ash	42mm sq × 1060mm long (1⁵/₈ in sq × 41³/₄ in long)
3	Front stretcher	1	Ash	54mm sq × 440mm long (2¹/₈ in sq × 17³/₈ in long)
4	Side/back stretcher	5	Ash	28mm sq × 380mm long (1¹/₈ in sq × 15in long)
5	Front seat rail	1	Ash	40 × 22 × 480mm long (1⁵/₈ × ⁷/₈ × 19in long)
6	Side seat rail	2	Ash	40 × 22 × 380mm long (1⁵/₈ × ⁷/₈ × 15in long)
7	Back seat rail	1	Ash	40 × 22 × 390mm long (1⁵/₈ × ⁷/₈ × 15 ³/₈ in long)
8	Wavy line slat	5	Ash	75 × 8 × 420mm long (3 × ⁵/₁₆ × 16 ¹/₂ in long)
9	Rush seat		Rush	1 bolt – enough for 2 seats

EAST ANGLIA HOLLOW-SEAT ARMCHAIR

A chair form that is unique to the East Anglia area of England is the so-called 'hollow seat' chair. These were made from square section timber joined together using mortise and tenon connections, and woodturned parts were only rarely used. These chairs were hence made by cabinet makers and not woodturners. They were made both as side chairs and armchairs, and the industry was largely centred in Norfolk. Only in isolated instances have chairs been recorded with the maker's name stamp.

The woods traditionally used to make them were elm, fruit woods, oak and occasionally walnut. The earliest chairs had flat seats, and as time progressed in the nineteenth century 'hollow seats' were introduced. The hollow seat was usually made from one thin plank of wood or occasionally two pieces, with the grain running from front to back. On early chairs you will sometimes find strips of hessian stuck on the underside with Scotch glue to strengthen the thin board against cracking, together with small wood blocks glued on the inside of the seat rails for additional support. The front legs were of square-section form tapering towards the floor. The back posts, also of square section, were cut to a curved profile above seat level.

CLASSICAL INFLUENCES

A notable feature of hollow seat chairs is that the makers were influenced by the classical designs of Chippendale, Hepplewhite and Sheraton, as shown in Fig 13.1. The chair backs, especially, had features reminiscent of these designers, but with a more restrained simplistic approach. Chairs with a Chippendale influence might have a wavy top rail with ear-pattern ends, and a pierced splat below as in (A). Those with a Hepplewhite style featured a 'camel's back' head rail and a pierced splat (B), while chairs in the Sheraton fashion had vertical reeded banister-style backs (C).

HOLLOW-SEAT ARMCHAIR DESIGN

The hollow-seat chair design featured here is based on an original dated about 1790-1830. It has all the classic features, including tapered front legs and square section stretchers. The back is of Sheraton style with a slightly arched crest rail, below which are four reeded banisters. In the original the frame is made of beech, and the seat is thought possibly to be either alder or mahogany.

CONSTRUCTION

One of the reasons I chose to include this hollow-seat chair design was because it primarily utilises only joinery techniques with mortise and tenon jointing. Thus if you do not have a woodturning lathe, you will still be able to make a chair, which is both attractive in appearance and comfortable to sit on. True, the hollow seat in the original was probably steamed, but details are given on how to do this, and how to make the chair even without using steaming techniques. If either of these proves difficult then a flat seat board can be fitted. In the one made here I chose to use elm for the frame and seat board, a more figurative wood than beech, but as mentioned above other temporate hardwoods can be utilised. One particular point to remember is that because the seat board is of hollow form, it is necessary for the side seat rails to slope down slightly about 1½ degrees from front to back to enable you to fit the board. This is because the front legs are set wider than the back posts.

The general arrangement is given in Fig 13.2, and details of the parts in Figs 13.3. It is recommended that you use an ordered approach, and prepare as much of the frame and its jointing as possible while the wood still remains square, and cut the rounded profiles after this has been done. Doing things this way makes the timber much easier to mark out, hold in a vice, and cut either by hand or machine.

Front Legs

1 Prepare 40mm (1⁵/₈ in) square stock for the front legs. Cut the haunched mortises either by hand or machine. Taper down the inside faces only after this work is completed.

Back Posts

2 The back post side profile is shown on a squared background for ease of transfer to the wood. In the front view the back post is parallel up to seat level, i.e. 38mm (1½ in) thick, and then tapers down on the inside face to 28mm (1⅛ in) where it joins the top rail. Use hand and/or machine methods to cut this to shape, then form the mortise slots, and end tenon at the top. It is more economic to cut the two posts from one wider piece of wood.

▼ *Fig. 13.1 Hollow-seat chair back styles.*

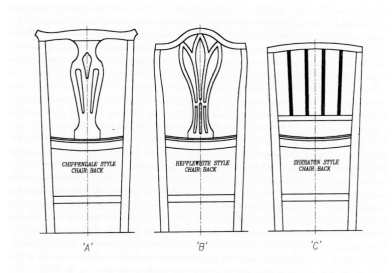

▶ Fig 13.2
*General
arrangement of
hollow-seat chair.*

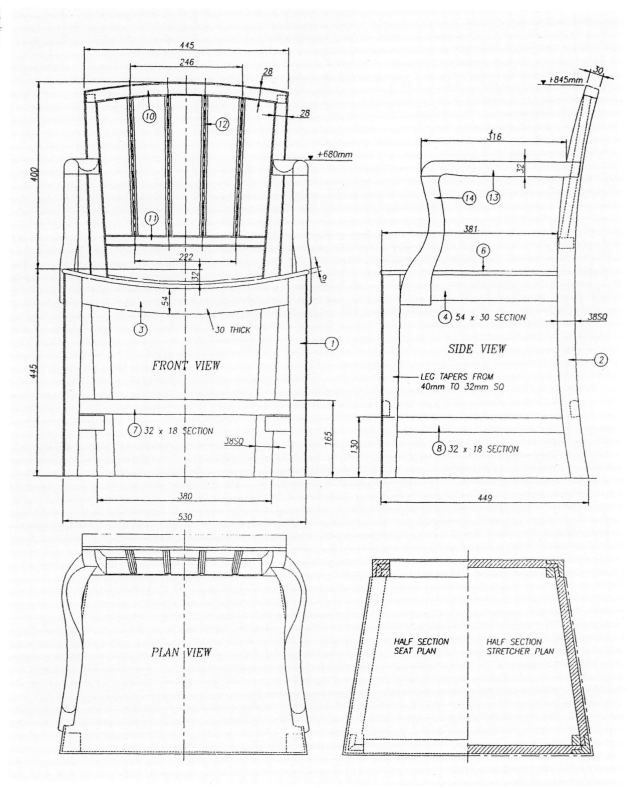

FRONT VIEW

SIDE VIEW

PLAN VIEW

HALF SECTION
SEAT PLAN

HALF SECTION
STRETCHER PLAN

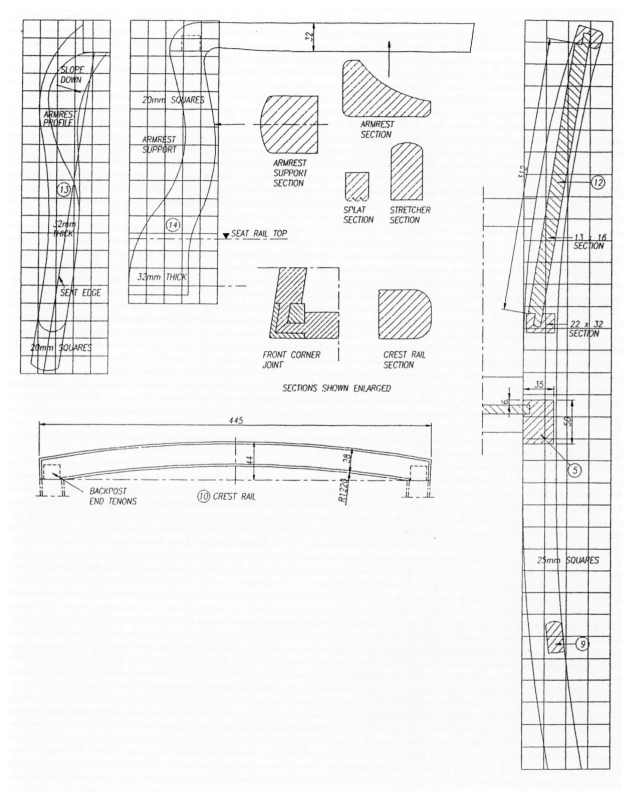

SLOPE DOWN

ARMREST PROFILE

(13)

32mm THICK

SEAT EDGE

20mm SQUARES

20mm SQUARES

ARMREST SUPPORT

(14)

▼ SEAT RAIL TOP

32mm THICK

32

ARMREST SECTION

ARMREST SUPPORT SECTION

SPLAT SECTION

STRETCHER SECTION

FRONT CORNER JOINT

CREST RAIL SECTION

SECTIONS SHOWN ENLARGED

445

44

28

BACKPOST END TENONS

(10) CREST RAIL

R1,220

◄ Fig 13.3
Hollow-seat chair details.

(12)

13 x 16 SECTION

22 x 32 SECTION

35

6

50

(5)

25mm SQUARES

(9)

Seat Rails

3 Prepare stock for the front, side and back seat rails of appropriate section, planed all round. These items are connected to the legs using haunched mortise and tenons. On the front and back rails, delay forming the hollow-seat profile until after the jointing has been completed. The jointing can be cut either by hand or by machine, e.g. using a radial arm saw, router and so on. The groove in the back rail for the seat board can also be cut by hand, but alternatively a router could be used mounted on a radius arm, or with suitable guides or templates.

Stretchers

4 Make the stretchers from 32 × 18mm (¹/₄ × ³/₄ in) section material of appropriate length planed all over. These are rounded over on the top surface. Again delay this operation until after the end tenons are finished. The latter are barefaced set to the inside.

Seat Board

5 The seat board is the most difficult part to make because it is a thin wide board, and also because of its curved profile. It is not easy to procure a thin planed board as wide as this, but if it is possible this is the ideal solution. If the board is too flat and needs hollowing slightly, I find that this can be done by placing it on top of the steaming Burco boiler with the lid off for about 10 to 30 seconds. As an alternative, try one of the following.

i   Make the seat board in three narrower strips. Steam these for half an hour and clamp them between shallow curved boards to shape them.

ii If steaming facilities are not available, but a hollow seat is required, make the three boards slightly over thick, and shape them with hand or machine tools to bed on to the seat rails.

iii Fit a flat seat board, either as one piece or in strips, depending on what timber is available. The front and back rails will need to be of parallel section rather than curved if this option is taken.

Banister Back

6 The banister back comprises the crest rail, middle rail and connecting reeded banisters. In making the crest rail, initially retain this as a square section to enable you first to mark and cut the mortise slots either end. Then cut it to a curved profile and form the intermediate banister mortises. Finally round over the back edges of this item. Cut the middle rail and banisters from straight planed material.

Armrests

7 Details of the armrests are given in Fig 13.3. These involve mainly handwork and a little careful shaping and carving. The profile is given on a squared background to enable transfer of the pattern to the wood. The armrest and its support are joined with a small mortise and tenon, and the latter has a local cut-out where it joins the side seat rail.

Decorative Beading

8 Decorative beading is applied to the outer corners of the front legs using a suitable scratchstock (Fig 13.4). This tool is also used to apply bead decoration to the inner and outer edges of the back posts, the crest and middle rails, and a reed effect on the front face of the four banisters (Fig 13.5). Some of this work can be done on the loose items, but where parts adjoin, e.g. the back post to the crest rail, this will have to be locally finished in situ when the chair frame is fitted together.

First Assembly

9 Initially assemble the whole chair dry without glue, to ensure all parts fit together satisfactorily. Fit together the front and back frames individually and check these are square and without wind, and that the mortise and tenon jointing is tight without gaps. If the mortise and tenons are hand cut, a feeler gauge can be useful to check the fit of these. This may sound silly, but by slipping a thin feeler under the shoulder of a tenon, say, where a seat rail beds down to a front corner leg, you can sense the high spots and locally remove these with a chisel.

10 Join the front and back frames with the side rails and stretchers, and check the chair stands firm on all four feet.

11 Add on the seat board and check this, or the pieces it comprises, bed well down and fit tightly together. On the original this is stuck down in one piece, but today it makes

▶ Fig 13.4
*Applying
decorative beading
with a
scratchstock.*

Staining and Finishing

13 On a chair of this type it is debatable at what stage to start staining, sealing and polishing. Certainly it will be possible to do some preliminary work, perhaps staining and sealing some of the surfaces excluding the joints. It makes sense to do this on areas where there are tight nooks and crannies which may be difficult to polish later.

Final Assembly

14 Finally glue the chair together in stages, repeating steps 9–13. Clean off any excess PVA glue using a damp cloth. Finish polishing any areas of the chair which need working on and buff all over with wax.

◂◂ *Fig 13.5 Chair back corner beading.*

◂◂ *Fig 13.6 Chair banister back assembled.*

more sense to fit this with button pieces underneath fitted into grooves in the seat rails. This way you reduce the risk of the seat board splitting due to humidity changes. This is especially necessary on the front and back rails where the grain of the seatboad is transverse to these rails.

12 Add on the armrest and its support and screw these roughly into place. Use brass screws if the chair frame is of oak.

PARTS LIST

Item	Description	No	Material	Dimensions
1	Front leg	2	Elm	40mm sq × 445mm long
				($1^{5/8}$ in sq × $15^{1/2}$ in long)
2	Back post	2	Elm	140 × 38 × 850mm long
				(for both)
				($5^{1/2}$ × $1^{1/2}$ × $33^{1/2}$ in long)
3	Front seat rail	1	Elm	85 × 30 × 530mm long rail
				($3^{3/8}$ × $1^{1/4}$ × 21in long)
4	Side seat rail	2	Elm	57 × 30 × 430mm long
				($2^{1/4}$ × $1^{3/16}$ × 17in long)
5	Back seat rail	1	Elm	65 × 35 × 420mm long
				($2^{1/2}$ × $1^{3/8}$ × 16in long)
6	Seat board	1	Elm	280 × 10 × 400mm long
				(2 pieces)
				(11 × $3/8$ × $15^{3/4}$ in long)
7	Front stretcher	2	Elm	32 × 18 × 530 long
				($1^{1/4}$ × $3/4$ × 21in long)
8	Side stretcher	1	Elm	32 × 18 × 430mm long
				($1^{1/4}$ × $3/4$ × 17in long)
9	Back stretcher	1	Elm	32 × 18 × 400mm long
				($1^{1/4}$ × $3/4$ × $15^{3/4}$in long)
10	Crest rail	1	Elm	45 × 28 × 450mm long
				($1^{3/4}$ × $1^{1/8}$ × $17^{3/4}$ in long)
11	Middle rail	1	Elm	32 × 22 × 440mm long
				($1^{1/4}$ × $7/8$ × $17^{3/8}$ in long)
12	Banister	4	Elm	16 × 12 × 345mm long
				($5/8$ × $1/2$ × $13^{5/8}$ in long)
13	Armrest	2	Elm	80 × 32 × 360mm long
				($3^{1/4}$ × $1^{1/4}$ × $14^{1/4}$ in long)
14	Armrest support	2	Elm	80 × 32 × 320mm long
				($3^{1/4}$ × $1^{1/4}$ × $12^{5/8}$ in long)

HOLLOW-SEAT STOOL

esides making hollow-seat chairs, East Anglian chair makers also made stools in this style, both of normal height and bar size. I was fortunate to come across an attractive hollow-seat stool from this area to complement the chair in Chapter 13, and the design is detailed here.

The evolution of stools in East Anglia follows a very similar pattern to chairs in this region; that is, they were mostly of framed construction with mortise and tenon jointing. The earliest had flat seats as in Fig 14.1 (A). Later the hollow seat top was introduced as in (B) although there was a fair degree of overlap. The legs were commonly of square or tapered square form, though stools were also made with turned legs with pronounced vase and bead turnings (C). On stools of joined construction, square-form stretchers were used, either with an 'H'-frame arrangement or perimeter-frame style, but those with turned legs tended not to have stretchers. The stools were most commonly made of elm but other woods, such as mahogany and yew, were also used.

The hollow-seat stool design here is taken from an original dating from about 1790–1840 (Fig 14.2). It has splayed square tapered legs, an 'H'-frame stretcher arrangement and is made of elm. Simple mortise and tenon jointing is used to connect the legs, rails and stretchers. This is except for the centre stretcher end connections, which are half-jointed with one edge of dovetail form to stop it pulling out. The end stretchers are set to the outside faces of the legs.

CONSTRUCTION

This again is a project which primarily uses only joinery and finishing skills, although you may need steam-bending techniques to assist in forming the hollow-seat board, depending on what approach you take to making this. Dimensional details of the stool

are given in Figs 14.2 and 14.3. I chose to make the replica of elm, but oak, yew or fruit woods would be good alternatives. As for the hollow-seat chair in Chapter 13, it pays to have an ordered approach, and to work on joints whilst the wood is retained square, rather than after it has been hollowed out or tapered, when it becomes more difficult to hold the timber in a vice, and cut by hand or machine.

Legs, Rails and Stretchers

1 Prepare square stock timber of appropriate section for the legs, side rails and stretchers, planed all round, and mark out the joints in readiness for cutting.

2 On the front and back rails, cut the haunched mortise and tenons before curving these to the hollow-seat form. Cut these either by hand or machine means, such as a radial arm saw, as appropriate. Taper the legs down only after the corner jointing is complete. Note the chamfer on the inside back edge of the legs.

3 Join the end stretchers to the legs with full height mortise and tenons. Make the centre stretcher with a half joint at either end, with one side cut with a dovetail edge.

Seat Board

4 The original seat top is of one-piece construction with the grain running front to back. Obtaining and bending a large piece of elm as thin as this may present problems, but if possible this is the preferred arrangement. The situation is similar to the hollow-seat chair in Chapter 13 where three alternative options were suggested. In this instance only the first two can

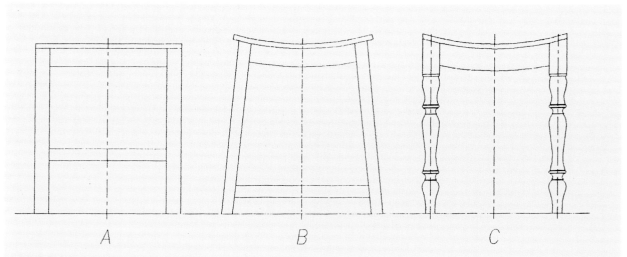

A   B   C

◀ Fig 14.1 East Anglian stools.

▶ Fig 14.2
General
arrangement
of stool.

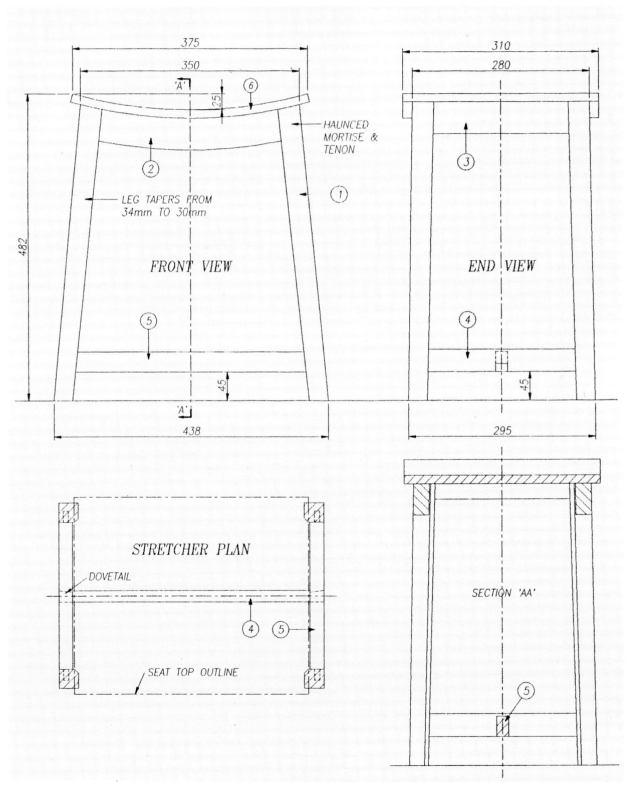

375

350

'A'

25

⑥

482

'A'

HAUNCED
MORTISE &
TENON

②

LEG TAPERS FROM
34mm TO 30mm

①

FRONT VIEW

⑤

45

438

310

280

③

END VIEW

④

45

295

STRETCHER PLAN

DOVETAIL

④ ⑤

SEAT TOP OUTLINE

SECTION 'AA'

⑤

really be used here, i.e. making the seat board in narrower strips, steam bent to shape, or cutting the strips over thick and shaping them by hand or machine to fit the hollow seat rails. The third suggestion of fitting a flat seat top is not really applicable because this does not suit the splayed taper leg style. However, you could redesign the stool so the tapered legs are vertical, in which case a flat seat board could be used.

Assembly

5   Fit the stool together initially dry without glue. First assemble the end frame items (1), (3) and (4), then link these together with the front and back rails (2), and finally fit the centre stretcher (5) in from underneath. If the joints are hand cut, use the feeler gauge technique suggested on page 78 to ensure the tenon shoulders are bedded tightly. Check that there is no wind on the end frames and that the stool stands firm on all four feet. Fit the seat board using button pieces underneath to minimise the risk of splitting because of humidity changes.

Finishing

6   Dismantle the stool and prefinish the components as much as possible, staining, sealing and polishing the surfaces, and keeping these clear of joint surfaces to be glued later. When this work is complete, glue the assembly together, and wipe off any excess PVA glue with a damp cloth. When the glue is set, refinish any parts needing treatment.

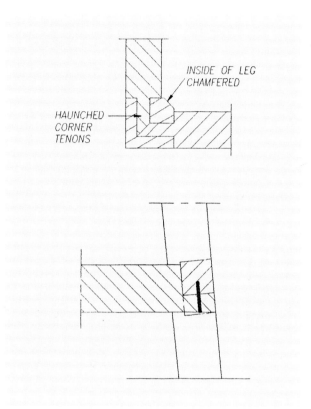

INSIDE OF LEG CHAMFERED

HAUNCHED CORNER TENONS

◀ Fig 14.3
Details of stool jointing.

PARTS LIST

Item	Description	No	Material	Dimensions
1	Leg	4	Elm	32mm sq × 482mm long (1¼in sq × 19in long)
2	Front rail	2	Elm	65 × 25 × 350mm long (2½ × 1 × 13¾in long)
3	End rail	2	Elm	50 × 25 × 280mm long (2 × 1 × 11in long)
4	End stretcher	2	Elm	36 × 22 × 280mm long (1⁷⁄₆ × ⁷⁄₈ × 11in long)
5	Centre stretcher	1	Elm	32 × 19 × 375mm long (1¼ × ¾ × 14¾in long)
6	Seat board	1	Elm	400 × 10 × 310mm wide (15¾ × ⅜ × 12¼in wide)

◀◀ Fig 14.4
Fitting the stool together.

NEW ENGLAND CHILD'S CHAIR

One of the interesting aspects about the evolution of regional chairs in America was the popularity there of painted surface finishes, whereas in Britain the tendency was more to emphasise the wood grain using transparent stains and lacquers. Painted finishes were especially popular in America between 1800 and 1845, and the design in this chapter is a typical example from this period. This is for a small child's armchair from New England and is based upon one that I came across from Sturbridge Village, Massachusetts. This, by the way, is an open-air museum similar to Ironbridge in England, and is a superb place to learn something about the early rural development and colonisation of America. The original chair c.1820 has vase-and-bead turning on the back posts, a rush seat, and hand-painted decoration on the slats. Before detailing the design let us look briefly at painted finishes as these relate to early American chairs.

PAINTING AND STENCIL DECORATION

The taste for painted finishes applied especially to American slat backs, rockers and fancy chairs and was popular during the first half of the nineteenth century. In the period between 1800–1845 these chairs were often additionally decorated with painted motifs such as floral patterns, leaves, fruit and vines. In the early years this was applied by hand painting and later after 1820 by stencilling, which eliminated the need for skilled artists in factory production. The base paint colours were mostly black, dark red and green, but other colours such as yellow, orange and brown were also used. Graining was also simulated mostly with black paint applied over red or yellow. Around 1830 transparent oil colours were introduced and these were painted over the stencilled flower patterns. The centre of flowers was often painted red. The regional variety is such that with an intimate knowledge of the type of base paint, the stencil style, and the colours used it is possible to date a chair and know its probable origin. For example, stencil patterns of grapevines intertwined with tendrils were very popular. A pattern with perhaps one or two stencilled tendrils might date from 1825, but a design with many tendrils would be slightly later, say, 1830.

ARMCHAIR DESIGN

In the child's armchair design here I have adopted as far as practical the woods and painted finishes, as would have been used for slat-back chairs at the time the original chair was made. In America the choice of woods used to make slat-back chairs varied but was to some extent dictated by what was locally available. For example, Maine and New Hampshire favoured birch, Massachusetts maple, and Connecticut poplar. In other areas woods such cherry, fruit woods, hickory, oak, chestnut and pine were used. Since a painted finish was being used, birch, a pale hardwood without much figure but more durable than pine was selected. With regard to the finish, as has been noted, American ladder-backs were traditionally painted

and from the primary choice of black, dark red and green the latter was selected. The floral decoration can either be painted or stencilled on to the slats.

CONSTRUCTION

This is a relatively easy project primarily involving spindle turning, some simple slat bending, and rush-seating skills. The longest spindle is 700mm (27in) so is well within the capabilities of the standard lathe. The chair design is slightly wider at the front relative to the back, though you could make it of square form if you wish. The general arrangement is shown in Fig 15.1 and details of the chair parts in Fig 15.2. The order of work is as follows.

Corner posts and stretchers

1 Prepare sawn timber for the front and back posts and stretchers.

2 Woodturn the front and back posts (1) and (2) to the dimensions in Fig 15.2. These items have attractive bead-and-vase turnings.

3 Machine the stretchers (5) and (6). If you choose to make a square form chair the lengths need not vary, but can all be the same as the back stretcher, i.e. 265mm (10^7/$_{16}$in).

4 Smooth these items ready for the painted finish applied later.

Seat Rails

5 The seat rails shown are of the conventional square section form, i.e. hand-cut pieces with machined ends. Alternatively you can woodturn these similar to the stretchers if desired. However there is a slight disadvantage when rush-seating over these in that the rush tends to slide along especially on the side rails. It is actually better for these rails to have a squarer form because it makes rush work easier.

Slats

6 Prepare material for the slats 6mm (^{1}/$_4$in) thick of suitable width and length and steam bend these to shape. While the bend need not be quite as much as for an adult chair, say, about 20mm (^{3}/$_4$in) the radius of curvature is smaller because of the reduced space between the back posts so you may need to put small packers under the ends in the slat press. Otherwise follow the instructions for steaming in Chapter 4. Bend the slats as a pair and remember to act swiftly in taking them from the steamer and cramping them.

7 When the slats are dry and set, clean these up and remove any mottled surface aberrations caused by the steaming process.

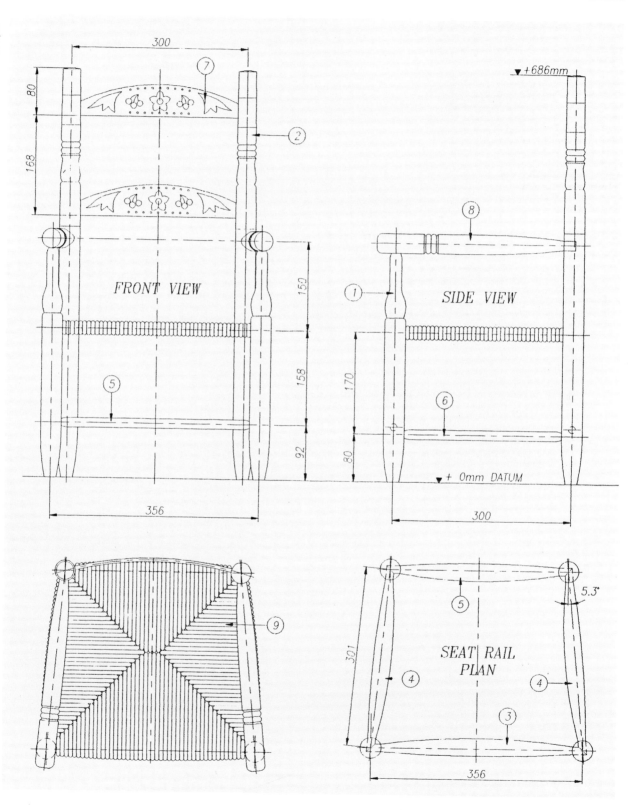

◀ Fig 15.2
Details of
chair parts.

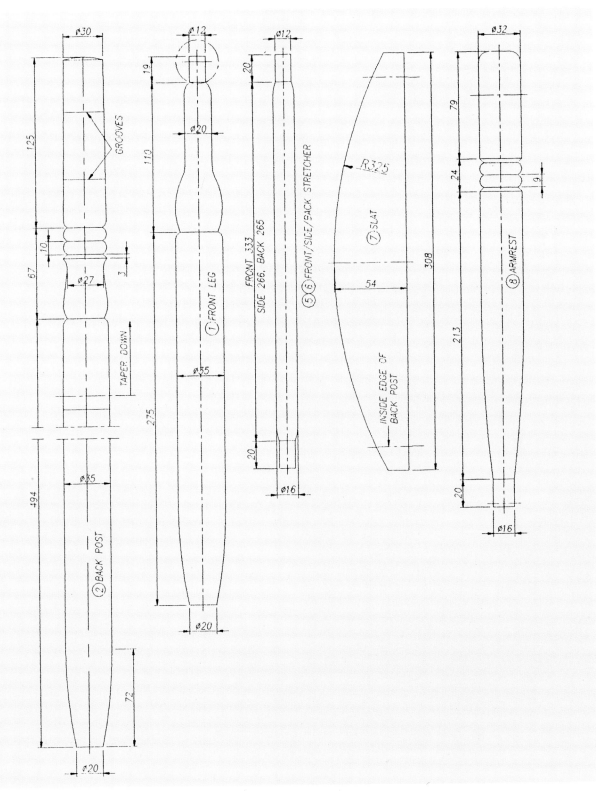

GROOVES

Ø30

125

67

10

Ø27

3

TAPER DOWN

Ø35

② BACK POST

494

72

Ø20

Ø12

19

Ø20

110

① FRONT LEG

Ø35

275

Ø20

Ø12

20

FRONT 333
SIDE 266, BACK 265

20

Ø16

⑤ ⑥ FRONT/SIDE/BACK STRETCHER

R325

⑦ SLAT

54

308

INSIDE EDGE OF
BACK POST

Ø32

79

24

9

⑧ ARMREST

213

20

Ø16

▶ *Fig 15.3*
Stencil pattern.

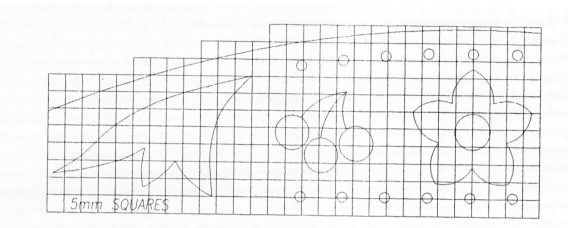

5mm SQUARES

▶ *Fig 15.4 Chair*
assembly.

9 For the slat mortises, assuming a bend of 20mm ($^3/_4$ in) the angle for these in the corner posts is approximately 15 degrees. However, the curvature you obtain may vary, and the best method is to trace the slat-edge profile on a piece of paper and measure the angle.

10 Cut the corner post slat mortises by chain drilling these under the drill press. Use the 'V' jig to position the legs under the drill press as under step 8 above. The mortises are offset approximately 3mm ($^1/_8$ in) towards the back of the corner posts. The slats should fit firmly with no visible gaps. Taper the slat tenons slightly on the back face where they enter the mortise, so that they can then be driven in nice and tight.

Assembly

11 Assemble the front and back frames individually, checking these are square and there is no wind.

12 Link the front and back frames together with the side rails and stretchers. Check the chair stands firmly on all four feet. Make minor corrections if necessary.

13 Glue the individual frames together, and then to each other. Recheck at each stage the frame and chair is square. Wipe off excess glue with a damp cloth.

14 Smooth over all surfaces ready for the paint finish.

Paint Finish and Floral Decoration

15 Finish the chair with a suitable paint application. The choice is a personal one but the chair here was finished with an undercoat followed by a glossy dark green top coat.

Corner Post Holes and Slots

8 Drill the 16mm ($^5/_8$ in) holes for the seat rails and stretchers using the 'V' jig (see page 17) to hold the legs and posts. The holes for the side seat rails and stretchers are offset approximately 5 degrees, but for a square-form chair, the offset is not needed.

16 Whether you stencil or hand-paint the floral decoration on the slats depends on the painted finish. You cannot easily stencil patterns on to a gloss surface, so if you choose this option, you must first matt down the gloss on the slats. Next prepare stencils from transparent card. The pattern for these is given in Fig 15.3. Use these with paint of appropriate colour to apply the pattern on to the slats. Then spray the slats with transparent lacquer to regloss the surfaces. The alternative – hand-painting – is quite easy. For this you need first to transfer the pattern using white carbon paper so it is clearly visible, and then use a fine sable brush to paint on the floral feature.

Rush Seating

17 The preferred method of finishing the seat is to use rush, but as an alternative for those wishing a quicker job, seagrass can be used. When rush seating remember that this is a child's chair so select thinner rushes to twist together. Rush suppliers will sometimes ask the intended application for the rush you are buying and will suggest a thinner grade if possible.

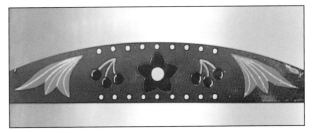

◀ Fig 15.5
Painted floral
decoration.

◀ Fig 15.6
Rush seat.

PARTS LIST

Item	Description	No	Material	Dimensions
1	Front leg	2	Birch	42mm sq × 430mm long (1⁵⁄₈ in sq × 17in long)
2	Back post	2	Birch	42mm sq × 715mm long (1⁵⁄₈ in sq × 28¹⁄₄in long)
3	Front seat rail	1	Birch	30 × 19 × 400mm long (1¹⁄₄ × ³⁄₄ × 15³⁄₄in long)
4	Side/back seat rail	3	Birch	30 × 19 × 340mm long (1¹⁄₄ × ³⁄₄ × 13¹⁄₂in long)
5	Front stretcher	1	Birch	22mm sq × 400mm long (⁷⁄₈in sq × 15 ³⁄₄in long)
6	Side/back stretcher	3	Birch	22mm sq × 340mm long (⁷⁄₈in sq × 13¹⁄₂in long)
7	Slat	2	Birch	54 × 6 × 350mm long (2¹⁄₈ × ¹⁄₄ × 14in long)
8	Armrest	2	Birch	42mm sq × 370mm long (1⁵⁄₈in sq × 14³⁄₄in long)
9	Rush seat	1	English rush	1 bolt – sufficient for 3 small child's seats

SHAKER SIDE CHAIR

Shaker furniture has always been held in high esteem and has been very popular in recent years. The design here for a Shaker side chair is typical of the refined style which evolved, and if we reflect for a moment on the history of the Shaker movement and its ideals, you will perhaps understand just how these chairs in some ways symbolise the Shaker virgin purity.

THE SHAKERS

The Shakers were a religious Utopian sect started by Mother Ann Lee in 1774, who believed in celibacy and called themselves the 'United Society of Believers of Christ's Second Appearing'. They became known as the Shakers because of their prayer meetings, during which they participated in erratic dancing and shaking movements. Their lives were based on the principles of order, harmony and utility. They had a number of maxims including, 'Put your hands to work and your hearts to God', and, 'Do your work as though you had a thousand years to live, and as if you were to die tomorrow'. At its peak in the 1840s the sect had over 6000 members living in self-sufficient communities situated mostly in New England, and Fig 16.1 shows the location of some of the better-known settlements.

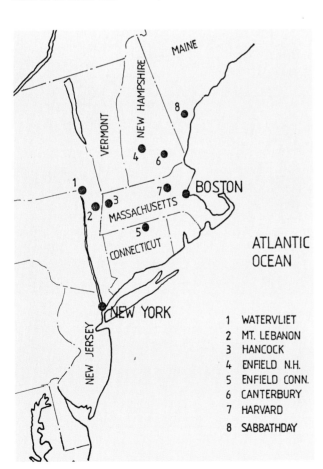

1	WATERVLIET
2	MT. LEBANON
3	HANCOCK
4	ENFIELD N.H.
5	ENFIELD CONN.
6	CANTERBURY
7	HARVARD
8	SABBATHDAY

SHAKER CHAIRS

Shaker furniture of course is well known, but it is the association with chair making for which the community is probably best remembered. What the Shakers did was to simplify the earlier New England slat-back chair, by making it of more slender proportions and removing the ornamental turning, to produce a finely structured chair of relatively light weight. A common feature was the use of mushroom-style hand holds adapted from pilgrim period armchairs. Indigenous woods such as American cherry, birch and maple were utilised to create a simple harmonious form. There was no place for exotic woods, or the use of embellishments such as carvings which would detract from this harmony. In effect this turned it into a highly refined country chair, which some see as an extension of Shaker spirituality.

Just as English vernacular furniture has developed strong regional traits, so too have Shaker chairs, and by studying these you can form a good idea from which settlement a chair might have originated. This means looking carefully at the style and pattern of the different chair elements, i.e. the pommels (finials), corner posts, back slats, rockers, armrests, seat and stretchers. Sometimes a single feature will be enough for you to make a judgement. The shape of pommels is an example; they tend to be characteristic to particular settlements, and just occasionally you will find a name stamp such as 'FW' (Freegift Wells) on them. More likely, though, the judgement will be based on a number of factors about the chair as a whole.

◀◀ *Fig 16.1 Shaker settlements.*

POSTS, POMMELS AND STRETCHERS

The posts on Shaker chairs are typically long and slender. The back posts had a finial called a 'pommel' formed at the top, and some of the variations in shape are given in Fig 16.2. I have grouped these pommels into rounded top, elliptic and candlewick/cone shaped. The rounded-top ones are (A) Canterbury, (B) Sabbathday and (C) Pleasant Hill. The more elliptic ones (D), (E) and (F) are from the Enfield and Harvard communities, and the cone-shaped pommels (G) and (H) are associated with North Union, and Mount Lebanon. Shaker stretchers typically taper slightly from the middle to the ends.

SLATS

Common slat forms which were used on Shaker chairs are shown in Fig 16.3. Mostly they have a curved top with a flat underside as in (A), and may be graduated in width from top to bottom. In a variation associated with Canterbury the lower slat edge is slightly down-curved as in (B). Another style is the wavy pattern slat with variants as in (C) and (D) seen in the North Union and Mount Lebanon communities. A shape with a scalloped end (D) is possibly also associated with North Union, Ohio. Sometimes the slats were fixed with a peg into the back posts. Shaker chairs were also made with a curved bar across the top reminiscent of the Macclesfield bar-top chair (see Chapter 11), which was supposedly designed to rest a cushion on.

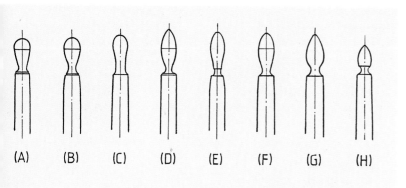

(A) (B) (C) (D) (E) (F) (G) (H)

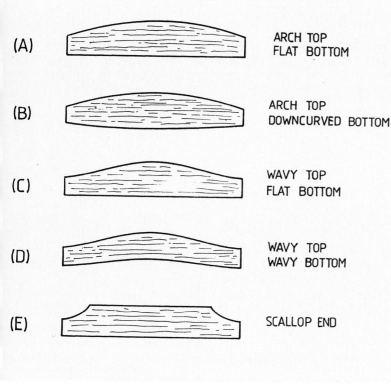

(A) ARCH TOP FLAT BOTTOM

(B) ARCH TOP DOWNCURVED BOTTOM

(C) WAVY TOP FLAT BOTTOM

(D) WAVY TOP WAVY BOTTOM

(E) SCALLOP END

▲ Fig 16.2 Shaker post pommels.

▲ Fig 16.3 Back slat forms.

CHAIR DESIGN

The Shaker side chair here is based on the style of the Canterbury settlement with a three-slat back. The back posts have rounded-top pommels. The seat is designed to suit an odd number of tapes for both warp and weft. This is so that a two-colour pattern, radiating from the centre, can be made if desired. The seat size depends on the braid width being used, which in this case was 25mm (1in).

CONSTRUCTION

The techniques you need to make the Shaker side chair are woodturning, joinery, tape weaving and, to a small extent, steam bending. The timber choice should ideally be one of those grown in the United States, such as American cherry, birch and maple. American cherry was used partly because as it matures it oxidises to a lovely nut brown colour. It is however a softer timber than the others, so has to be treated with care to avoid bruising. Purchase the seat tape before you start as the width sometimes varies depending on the source, and this can affect the distance between the front and back posts slightly. The general arrangement is given in Fig 16.4, and details of parts in Fig 16.5.

Front Legs and Back Posts

1　Prepare bandsawn material 45mm (1³/₄ in) square for the front and back posts. These are turned end to end in accordance with the measurements given. The finished diameter of these is 38mm (1¹/₂ in). Some Shaker chair posts were as small as 32–35mm (1¹/₄–1³/₈ in) in diameter, which is a little on the slender side for accepting reasonable size holes for the stretcher ends, though you could try it if you like. A lathe steady will be needed to minimise vibration during machining of the back posts.

Rails and Stretchers

2　Cut 28mm (1¹/₈ in) square section material for the 12 rails and stretchers. Woodturn the seat rails so these are parallel, and the stretchers with a slight taper down from the middle finishing with the dowel ends.

Slats

3　Make the slats from planed material 6mm (¹/₄ in) thick of the specified width. Steam these together for 20 minutes, then bend them as a pack under the slat press, and allow them to dry and set, following the procedure detailed in Chapter 4. For a bend of 32mm (1¹/₄ in) the former needs to accommodate about 45mm (1³/₄ in) curvature, allowing for spring back. Cut them to shape afterwards using a bandsaw with a paste-on paper pattern to act as a guide. Clean them up to remove any mottled aberrations.

SEAT FORMS

Shaker chairs used woven seats, and wood splint and cotton tape were the two most common materials employed, though others such as leather, cane and rush were also used. The earliest chairs, made before 1830, tended to use wood splint. Colourful woven tape seats usually had a plain tabby weave, but sometimes other patterns were adopted. After 1850 there was a tendency to adopt tapes of a single colour. The Shakers used a revolving jig to hold the chair at the mid point of the back posts, so that it could be easily swivelled round. The seat weaver was thus always working on the top surface.

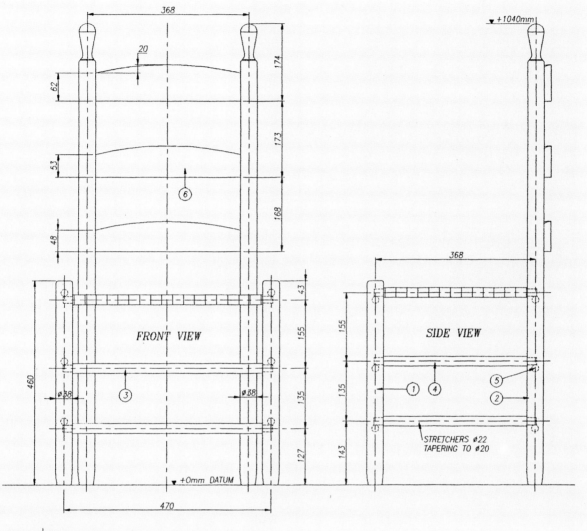

FRONT VIEW

SIDE VIEW

STRETCHERS ø22
TAPERING TO ø20

+0mm DATUM

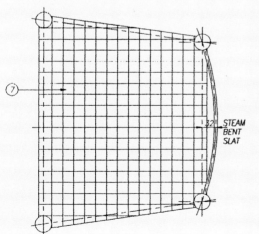

STEAM
BENT
SLAT

Corner Post Holes and Mortises

4 Use the 'V' jig (see page 17) to drill the 16mm (⁵/₈in) holes
   in the front legs and back posts, to fit the seat rails and
   stretchers. The holes for the side seat rails and stretchers
   are offset approximately 4 degrees at either side. Mark the
   holes accurately and check before drilling that you have
   got them right.

5   Assuming a slat bend of 32mm (1¹/₄in) the slat mortises in
    the back posts are offset approximately 18 degrees set
    towards the back about 6mm (¹/₄in) behind centre. As this
    depends partly on the actual curvature, it is best to trace the
    slat-edge profile on a piece of paper first and measure this.

▶ *Fig. 16.5*
Details of Shaker
side chair.

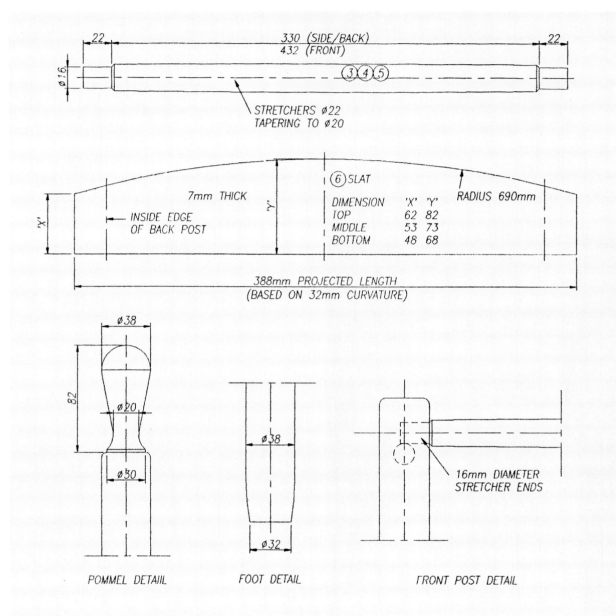

First Assembly

6   After all parts are made and cleaned up, assemble the chair initially without glue. Fit together the front and back frames individually, and check these are square and without wind. Then link these two frames together with the adjoining seat rails and stretchers, and check the chair stands squarely on the floor.

Finishing

7   Dismantle and prefinish the items as much as possible, keeping sealer and polish away from the areas to be glued. A stain is not appropriate for American cherry but if you use birch or maple, you might consider this.

Final Assembly

8   Glue the chair together following the order and alignment checks as in step 6 above. Wipe off any excess glue with a damp cloth. When the glue is set, refinish any areas needing further treatment.

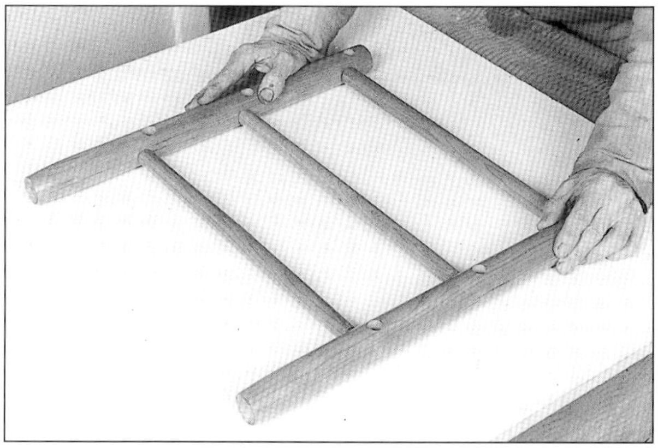

◂◂ *Fig 16.6 Chair front frame.*

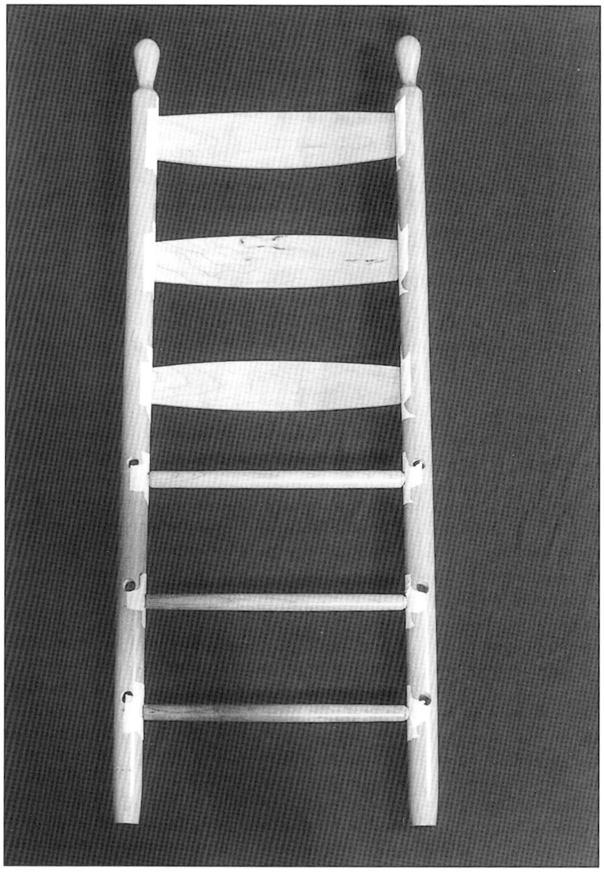

◂◂ *Fig 16.7 Chair back frame.*

Seat Weaving

8 The seat braid width is normally 25mm (1in) but there is no reason why you should not use a different width providing the space between the posts is adjusted accordingly. In weaving the seat tape, the warp is first wrapped back and forth round the front and back stretchers, and the ends are fixed with tacks. Extra warp strips are then tacked on either side to accommodate the additional width of the front legs. Although you want a nice firm seat, be careful not to over tension the warp. This is because when you thread in the weft in, it tends to tighten the warp even more, and in the extreme can deform the stretchers at the mid point. Before you add the weft, insert a piece of wadding or foam rubber between the warp. This will make the seat more comfortable.

Parts List

Item	Description	No	Material	Dimensions
1	Front leg	2	American cherry	45mm sq x 500mm long (1¾in sq x 19¾in long)
2	Back post	2	American cherry	45mm sq x 1080mm long (1¾in sq x 42½ in long)
3	Front rail/stretcher	3	American cherry	28mm sq x 440mm long (1⅛in sq x 7⅜in long)
4	Side rail/ stretcher	6	American cherry	28mm sq x 400mm long (1⅛in sq x 15¾in long)
5	Back rail/stretcher	3	American cherry	28mm sq x 400mm long (1⅛in sq x 15¾in long)
6	Slat	3	American cherry	85 x 6 x 410mm long (3⅜ x ¼ x 16¼in long)
7	Seat tape	1	Cotton web	25mm (1in) wide

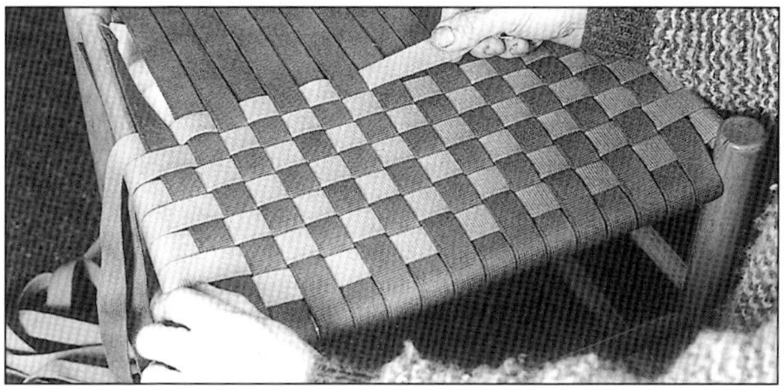

◂ *Fig 16.8 Tape seat weaving.*

SHAKER ROCKING CHAIR

Besides making side chairs the Shaker community produced a wide variety of other types including armchairs, bar tops, stools, settees, child's chairs, high chairs, and even stick-back revolving chairs. However, the type for which they were most famed is the rocking chair, with its unique 'inset' form of rocker. The design here is for one based on the style of the Mount Lebanon, Settlement, New York. This design was made in a range of sizes designated 0 to 7, the smallest for children and the larger ones for adults.

ROCKERS

As just mentioned Shaker rockers are 'inset' rather than set on, and Fig 17.1 shows nine common forms, together with the settlements with which they are associated. It is hard to imagine a wider variation. You would think that a comparison of the style with the location of the settlement might reveal some similarity with communities who lived nearer to each other, but this does not seem to be so. A unique method of rocking a chair peculiar to the Shakers is the tilter, consisting of an half ball set into the foot of the back post, and held in place by a leather thong.

ARMRESTS

By their nature rocking chairs tend to have armrests, the support for which is usually provided by an extension of the front leg, and the Shakers used three basic styles as shown in Fig 17.2. These were the vertical scroll (A), and the sideways scroll with a mushroom top as in (B) and (C). Vertical scroll armrests tend to be associated with Enfield NH, Canterbury and Harvard, and the sideways scroll with most of the others, but with arms of differing profile. The mushroom top, made as an extension of the front post, is often related with Enfield Conn. It requires wood of a large diameter, so much is wasted in woodturning. There is an

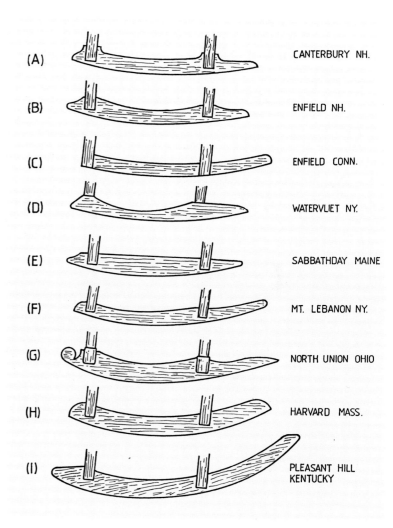

(A) CANTERBURY NH.

(B) ENFIELD NH.

(C) ENFIELD CONN.

(D) WATERVLIET NY.

(E) SABBATHDAY MAINE

(F) MT. LEBANON NY.

(G) NORTH UNION OHIO

(H) HARVARD MASS.

(I) PLEASANT HILL KENTUCKY

▲ Fig 17.1
Shaker rockers.

◀ Fig 17.2
Shaker armrests.

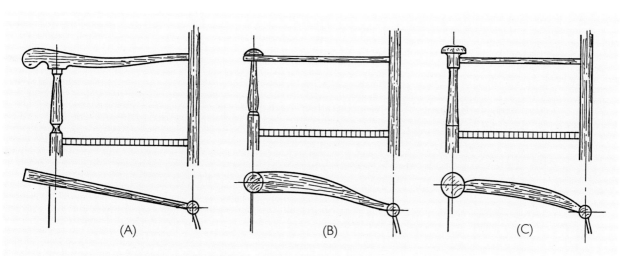

(A)   (B)   (C)

example of one of these in the American Museum in Britain. With regard to the pattern of the front leg supporting the armrest above the seat, this varied but a gentle tapering shape, or a vase shape of differing style, was commonly used.

SHAKER ROCKING CHAIR

The rocking chair design features a four-slat back with armrests and rockers based on the Mount Lebanon transitional NY style dating from around 1870. The chair has twin stretchers to the front, side and back, and the seat is woven with cotton braid.

CONSTRUCTION

The skills you need to make the Shaker rocking chair are woodturning, joinery, seat braid weaving and steam bending for the slats. The timber choice should ideally be an American one, such as maple, birch or American cherry. As recommended for the Shaker side chair, purchase the seat tape before commencing work as the width occasionally varies. The general arrangement is given in Fig 17.4 and details of the parts in Fig 17.3.

Front Legs and Back Posts

1 Cut bandsawn material 45mm (1³/₄in) square for the front legs and back posts, and machine these in accordance with the drawings. A lathe steady will be needed to minimise vibration during machining of the back posts and possibly also for the front legs.

Rails and Stretchers

2 Prepare 28mm (1¹/₈ in) square stock for the seat rails and stretchers. Turn the seat rails with a parallel section and the stretchers so they taper slightly in towards either end.

Slats

3 Prepare 6mm (¹/₄ in) thick planed material of appropriate width for the four slats. Steam these for 20 minutes, then bend them as a pack under the slat press. For a bend of 32mm (1¹/₄ in) the mould curvature needs to be about 45mm (1³/₄ in) to allow for spring back. Cut them to profile afterwards using a paste-on paper pattern as a saw guide.

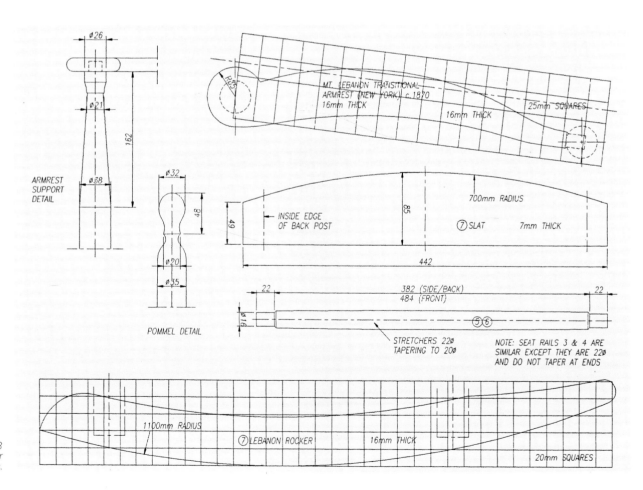

► Fig 17.3
Details of Shaker
chair parts.

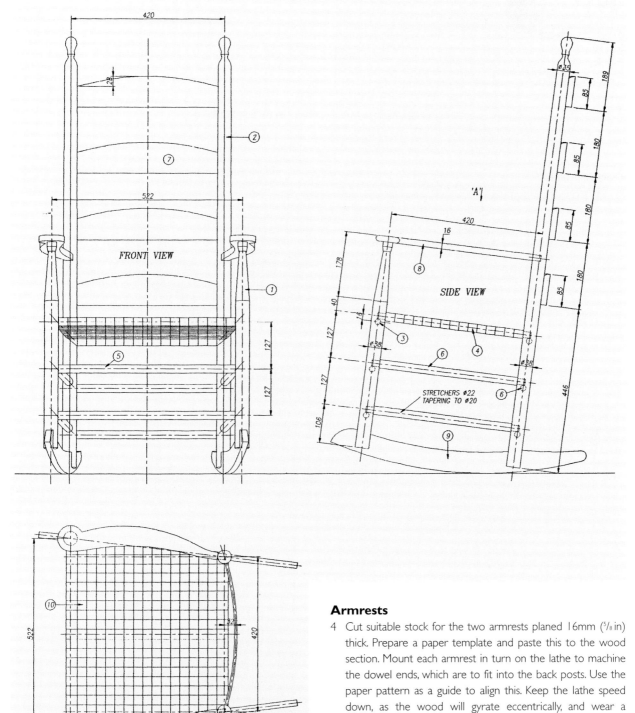

◀ Fig 17.4
General
arrangement
of Shaker
rocking chair.

Armrests

4   Cut suitable stock for the two armrests planed 16mm (⁵⁄₈ in)
thick. Prepare a paper template and paste this to the wood
section. Mount each armrest in turn on the lathe to machine
the dowel ends, which are to fit into the back posts. Use the
paper pattern as a guide to align this. Keep the lathe speed
down, as the wood will gyrate eccentrically, and wear a
protective visor during this operation. Remove the armrest
from the lathe and cut away the rest of the waste material
with a coping saw or a bandsaw. Sandpaper the surfaces in
readiness for polishing.

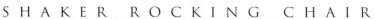

▶ *Fig 17.5*
Armrest pattern.

▶▶ *Fig 17.6 Fitting*
slats to backposts.

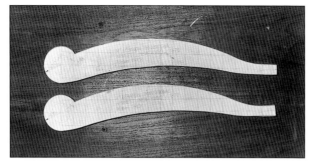

Rockers

5 Prepare the material planed for the two rockers. Initially leave these slightly over thick so that they can be thinned later if necessary and married more easily to the slots to be cut in the ends of the back posts. At this stage leave the rocker blanks square so they remain easily grippable in the vice, and do not cut them to the curved profile.

Corner Post Holes, Mortises and Slots

6 Use the 'V' jig (see page 17) to machine the holes in the front legs and back post for the stretchers and seat rails. You should also cut the end slots for the rockers at this stage. The post holes for the side rails and stretchers are offset 7 degrees either side. Be sure to align the holes correctly under the drill press.

7 Chain drill the mortise slots for the slat again using the 'V' jig. The slot angle is approximately 15 degrees, set about 5mm (³/₁₆ in) towards the back assuming a slat bend of 32mm (1¹/₄ in). To be accurate, draw the slat-edge profile on a piece of paper and use this as a guide.

First Assembly

8 Dry assemble the front and back frames individually and check these are square and without wind. Make sure the slats are a good tight fit, paring wood from the tenon ends on the back faces if needed. Connect the front and back frame together with the side rails and stretchers, fitting the armrests also at this point. Check the chair stands firmly on a level floor.

9 Upend the chair to fit the rockers. Place suitable protective material on the back posts and on other parts as necessary so the chair does not get damaged during this operation.

10 Prepare a straight planed strip of wood slightly thinner than the width of the rocker slots in the end of the front legs ,and back posts. Place this into each pair of slots to check they are aligned to each other. Clean up the slots where necessary, then offer the rockers into these. As at step 5,

the rockers should still be square and slightly over-thick. Plane the sides down in stages until they fit neatly in the slots. After the rocker blanks are fitted, remove them and paste on paper patterns to enable you to saw cut these to the profile as in Fig 17.3.

Finishing

11 Dismantle the chair and seal and polish the chair parts as far as practicably possible. As an alternative, it is worth mentioning that not all Shaker chairs were finished with polishes and waxes to enhance the natural wood grain. Some were painted in paler shades of blue, green and rustic red, occasionally picked out with contrasting lines, for example in mustard yellow. This is another option that you might consider when making the chair, and if so the painting can be done at a later stage after gluing up.

Fig 17.7 Aligning the corner rocker slots.

Final Assembly

12 Reassemble the rocking chair, this time with glue, checking for wind and squareness. Use a damp cloth to wipe off any surplus glue and refinish any surfaces needing treatment.

Tape Seat

13 The seat is woven with 25mm (1in) tape in a similar manner to the Shaker side chair. Begin by looping the warp over the front and back seat rails, filling in the corners with extra pieces tacked on. Then weave the weft crossways in and out. Remember to insert a piece of wadding or sheet foam between the warp to make the seat more comfortable. Check all the ends are neatly secured, give the chair a final inspection and wax the wood surfaces.

Fig 17.8 Assembled chair without rockers.

Parts List

Item	Description	No	Material	Dimensions
1	Front leg	2	American Cherry	45mm sq x 600mm long (1 3/4 in sq x 23 3/4in long)
2	Back post	2	American Cherry	45mm sq x 1210mm long (1 3/4 in sq x 47 3/4in long)
3	Front seat rail	1	American Cherry	28mm sq x 540mm long (1 1/8 in sq x 21 1/2 in long)
4	Side/back seat rail	3	American Cherry	28mm sq x 440mm long (1 1/8 in sq x 17 1/2in long)
5	Front stretcher	2	American Cherry	28mm sq x 540mm long (1 1/8 in sq x 21 1/2 in long)
6	Side/back stretcher	6	American Cherry	28mm sq x 440mm long (1 1/8 in sq x 17 1/2 in long)
7	Slat	4	American Cherry	90 x 6 x 440mm long (3 1/2 x 1/4 x 17 1/2 in long)
8	Armrest	2	American Cherry	90 x 16 x 460mm long (3 1/2 x 5/8 x 18 1/8 in long)
9	Rocker	2	American Cherry	100 x 16 x 720mm long (4 x 5/8 x 28 1/2 in long)
10	Tape seat	1	Cotton tape 25mm (1in) width	

PLATFORM ROCKING CHAIR

The platform rocking chair was introduced during the second half of the nineteenth century and was at the peak of popularity during the 1880s. It is essentially regarded as an American invention, though there are many Victorian examples in Britain too. It is so called because the rocker attached to the seat does not rest directly upon the floor, but instead sits on a platform that rests on the floor. The two are attached by a strong coil spring connection in between, one on either side. The idea was that by having a fixed rocker base the carpet beneath would not wear out so rapidly, as the rocking motion took place between the rocker and the raised platform. It is doubtful, however, if this really worked, especially as some were fitted with castors, which localised the wear problem. The design did, however, overcome the tendency of the rocker to creep, which occurs with ordinary rocking chairs if they are rocked back and forth energetically.

As for the springs, it was found that chairs that were fitted with a single coil on either side did not work very effectively, particularly if they were too springy. This was because they tended to let the rocker bounce back and forth too energetically, and this led to improved patent designs incorporating two springs. An American patent by W.I. Bunker on April 22, 1884, reference No. 297, was for a double-spring attachment for a platform rocking chair similar to that in Fig 18.1. This worked on the principle that as one spring was compressed, the other was extended. This was much more effective in limiting chair wobble.

Some of the firms who made this type of chair included the Enterprise Chair Manufacturing Co., Oxford, N.Y. (c. 1885); Sullivan & Co., N.Y., whose chairs retailed at $5.00 each; and a factory in Boston, Massachusetts, which produced in the 1880s upholstered chairs with the best Wilton carpet, retailing between $3.00 and $4.00. As mentioned earlier, they were sometimes made mounted on four castors or with castors at the front only. Despite their popularity the design necessitated a long base unit that could occasionally get in the way.

Because of the creaking nature of the spring unit and the rocking of wood on wood, they were not quite as noiseless as the chairs with rockers resting directly on a carpeted floor. However, some manufacturers apparently solved this by clever design. The woods used for construction were oak, more ornate timbers such as mahogany and walnut, and other woods that could be finished with a mahogany effect. The upholstered edge of the front seat sometimes had a tasselled finish. The chairs were made for both adults and children.

PLATFORM ROCKING CHAIR DESIGN

This chair design is based on an original with a fixed-platform base. It has turned members, featuring barrel, bead and vase turnings, and the seat and back are upholstered with a tapestry-style cloth.

CONSTRUCTION

The techniques needed to make this chair are woodturning, joinery and some fairly simple upholstery. The general arrangement is given in Fig 18.2 and details of the parts in Figs 18.3, 18.4 and 18.5. The suggested woods are those just mentioned, i.e. oak, walnut and mahogany, or others that will take a mahogany colour stain.

Turned items

1   The great majority of items for this chair are woodturned. Eighteen parts are required for the seat and armrest components, nine for the chair back, and four stretchers for the rocker base. Cut and prepare material for these items, and machine these to the dimensions given, with all dowel ends completed ready for joining the parts together.

2   While the work is lathe mounted, do as much finishing work as possible before machining off the ends.

Rockers and platform base

3   Prepare 35mm (1³⁄₈in) thick stock for the rockers (13) and the base platforms (14), and mark the patterns on the timber, including the positions for the rocker stretcher ends (15). Cut these out with a bandsaw, and clean up the surfaces by hand and/or machine. A belt sander and drum sander are useful aids for this work, especially for the concave surfaces. Drill the 19mm (³⁄₄in) blind holes for the stretchers.

◀◀ Fig 18.1
Double spring for a platform rocking chair.

▶ *Fig 18.2*
General
arrangement
of platform
rocking chair.

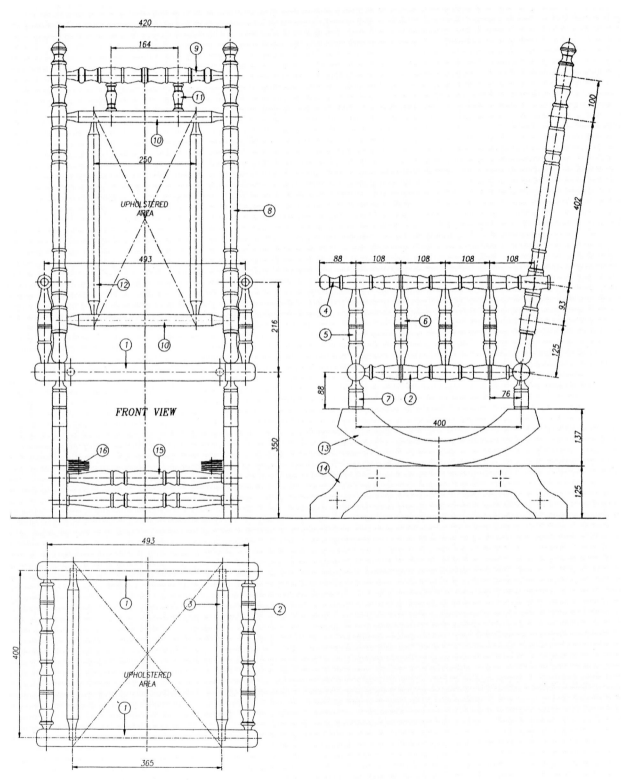

◀ Fig 18.3 Back details of platform rocking chair.

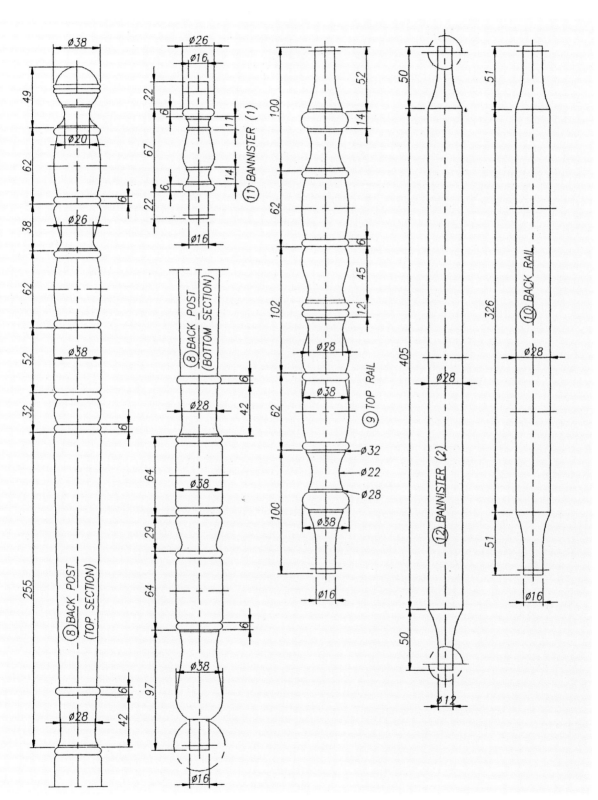

⑧ BACK POST (TOP SECTION)

⑧ BACK POST (BOTTOM SECTION)

⑪ BANNISTER (1)

⑨ TOP RAIL

⑫ BANNISTER (2)

⑩ BACK RAIL

▶ *Fig 18.4 Seat details of platform rocking chair.*

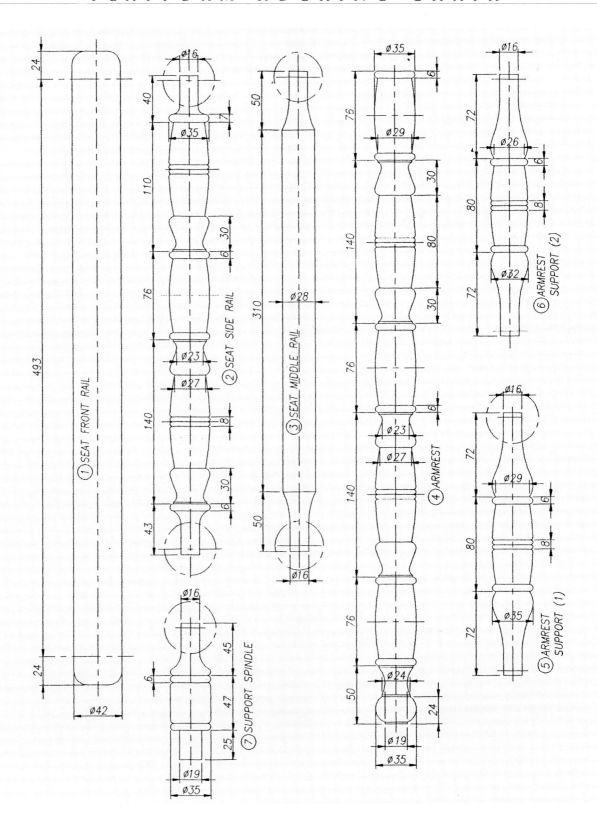

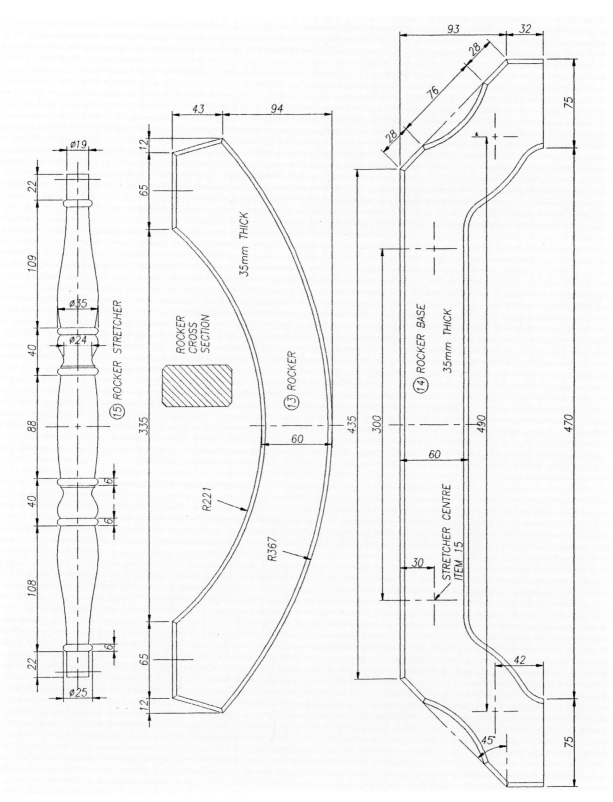

◀ Fig 18.5
Rocker details of
platform rocking
chair.

ROCKER
CROSS
SECTION

15 ROCKER STRETCHER

13 ROCKER

14 ROCKER BASE

35mm THICK

35mm THICK

STRETCHER CENTRE
ITEM 15

R221

R367

Fig 18.6 Chair seat assembly.

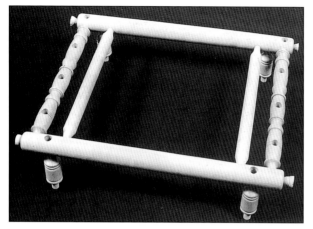

4 Apply the edge chamfer, 6mm ($^1/_4$ in), with a router using a 45-degree cutter with a guide pin. The router can either be hand-held or table-mounted for this operation, with the wood being firmly secured if the first option is used. Consult routing manuals for details of routing and safety procedures.

Drilling holes

5 Use the 'V' jig (see page 17) to drill the dowel holes in the various components. With the exception of the holes for the back posts into the rear seat rails, these are all 90 degrees drilled squarely through the turned items. Use Forstner or saw tooth bits to drill the holes cleanly. The only critical area is where the back posts (8) and the support spindles (7) join the rear seat rail. The holes for these meet in the middle, those for the back posts being offset approximately 9 degrees. As it is a through hole, this is the weakest joint in terms of chair frame strength, though with the other connecting parts the structure is sufficiently strong. Because these holes are slightly angled to one another, do make sure they meet in the middle and are not drilled over deep. The reason for this is that besides leaving voids on either side, which weakens the seat rail unnecessarily at this point, the dowel ends will also lack glue adhesion in these areas.

Fig 18.7 Base frame assembly.

First assembly

6 Commence assembly by joining the seat frame together as per Fig 18.2, i.e. front and back rails (1), and the side and middle rails (2), (3). Check for squareness and there is no wind. Add on the armrest supports (5) and (6). Check the armrest (4) will fit over the ends of the supports but do not fix for the moment.

7 Fit together the chair back items (8), (9), (10), (11) and (12), checking the chair width dimension is 420mm (16$^1/_2$ in). Add on the armrests (4), which fit to the back posts with short pieces of dowel via blind holes drilled in these items. Offer this

assembly carefully to fit into the seat back rail holes, gently easing the armrest down on to the ends of the armrest supports as you do this. You may need to sand the dowels down slightly to get the parts to fit on to each other.

8 Add the spindle supports (7) and the rockers (13).

9 Build up the rocker platform base unit comprising items (14) and (15), and decide where the spring units are to be screwed on.

Finishing

10 Dismantle the chair to continue staining, sealing and polishing those parts of the chair not previously completed at the machining stage, especially the rockers and platform base. Keep all finishing materials off those surfaces that will be glued later.

Final assembly

11 Reassemble the chair following through steps 6 to 9, checking for squareness at each stage. Wipe off excess PVA glue with a damp cloth, and refinish any areas needing treatment. Screw on the double spring units on either side.

Upholstery

12 For the upholstery you will need 50-mm (2-in) wide webbing. Tack or staple pieces of webbing on the inside face of the front rail. Wrap this round the front and over the back rail, tacking again on the underside of this. Fit three or four pieces as desired. Similarly staple webbing across the middle rails (3), weaving these in between the front to back webbing. Make sure the webbing is tight without any slack. Over the top of this, fit a piece of hessian, again tacked or stapled to the rails.

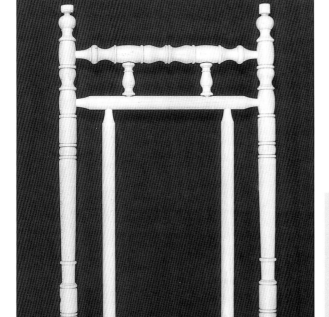

13 Select a suitable seat covering. In this instance I picked a tapestry pattern material. Remember to centralise this if you chose one with a pattern. Fold over the edges about 50mm (2in) to make a wide hem and oversew these. This hem must be wide enough to pass over the edges of the seat rails, so it can be tacked in place on the inside edges similar to the webbing. Fit this cover over the seat, inserting wadding in between over the hessian cover and then staple this in place.

14 Upholster the back in a similar manner to the seat, covering the tacks with a suitable edge fringe.

◀◀ *Fig 18.8 Chair back frame.*

PARTS LIST

Item	Description	No	Material	Dimensions
1	Front/back seat rail	2	Oak	50 mm sq × 580mm long (2 in sq × 23 in long)
2	Side seat rail	2	Oak	42 mm sq × 430mm long (1⁵⁄₈ in sq × 17in long)
3	Seat middle rail	2	Oak	35 mm sq × 440mm long (1³⁄₈ in sq × 17³⁄₈ in long)
4	Armrest	2	Oak	45 mm sq × 590mm long (1³⁄₄ in sq × 23¼ in long)
5	Armrest support (1)	2	Oak	42 mm sq × 240mm long (1⁵⁄₈ in sq × 9½ in long)
6	Armrest support (2)	4	Oak	42 mm sq × 240mm long (1⁵⁄₈ in sq × 9½ in long)
7	Support spindle	4	Oak	42 mm sq × 130mm long (1⁵⁄₈ in sq × 5⅛ in long)
8	Back post	2	Oak	45 mm sq × 850mm long (1³⁄₄ in sq × 33½ in long)
9	Top rail	1	Oak	45 mm sq × 440mm long (1³⁄₄ in sq × 17³⁄₈ in long)
10	Back rail	2	Oak	35 mm sq × 440mm long (1³⁄₈ in sq × 17³⁄₈ in long)
11	Banister (1)	2	Oak	32 mm sq × 130mm long (1¼ in sq × 5⅛ in long)
12	Banister (2)	2	Oak	32 mm sq × 440mm long (1¼ in sq × 17³⁄₈ in long)
13	Rocker	2	Oak	140 × 35 × 500mm long (5½in × 1³⁄₈in × 19¾in long)
14	Rocker base	2	Oak	125 × 35 × 630mm long (5 × 1³⁄₈ × 25in long)
15	Rocker stretcher	4	Oak	42 mm sq × 460mm long (1⁵⁄₈ in sq × 18⅛ in long)
16	Spring unit	2	Spring steel	Double spring unit
17	Upholstery	–	Webbing & material	50mm (2in) webbing, hessian and cover material

◀◀ *Fig 18.9 Upholstery.*

WEST MIDLANDS CORNER CHAIR

In the nineteenth century the West Midlands counties of Herefordshire, Worcestershire and Shropshire were home to a small group of chair makers producing wooden seated chairs in a distinct regional style. Notable chair makers in this area were the Clissetts, Coles, Warenders and Kerrys. Philip Clissett, in particular, was descended from a long line of chair makers. His father, Moses, had another son Cyrus, who later had two children, one also named Cyrus and the other Mary. They were all chair makers in the Clissett tradition. Philip's sons, John and William, continued in the chair-making tradition, although William died quite suddenly when he was 21. William Cole, a brother-in-law of Philip, also made chairs in a similar regional style. Philip Clissett lived at Stanley Hill, Bosbury, near Ledbury, and stamped his chairs 'P.C.' on the top end of the back posts. The Kerrys were based in Evesham, and the Warenders, who produced similar designs to the Clissetts, worked from Gilberts Lane, Bransford.

SEATS, STRETCHERS AND SPINDLE PATTERNS

These craftsmen made spindle-back, ladder-back and bar-top chairs constructed of ash and elm. They were characterised by thin elm wood seats which fitted into a groove cut in the woodturned side and back rails, and the front rail was a shaped board typically as in Fig 19.1. Chairs with rush seats were, however, also made in this area. Some examples of regional styles of stretchers and spindles are shown in Figs 19.2 and 19.3. The spindle type (c) is known to be associated with Philip Clissett. The cow-bell foot detail in Fig 19.3, seen on front and back posts, again is typical of chairs produced in this area.

CORNER CHAIR DESIGN

This West Midlands corner chair design is from an original in the High Wycombe chair museum and has typical regional features. Made of ash, it has a cabriole front leg with a pad foot, and three corner posts which have a bead detail above the seat and cow-bell form foot. Between these are fitted profiled and plain stretchers, those at the front having a type 'A' pattern (Fig 19.2). Above the rush seat is a semicircular armrest with pad-form ends, and the spindle back is formed by two rows of style 'A' spindles (Fig 19.3) fitting into curved rails.

CONSTRUCTION

The skills needed to make this chair are woodturning, joinery, steam bending for the middle rails, and rush weaving for the seat work. An alternative simpler slat-back design is also offered in place of the spindle back for a slightly easier construction. The general arrangement is given in Fig 19.4, and details of the parts in Figs 19.5, 19.6 and 19.7. The suggested order of work is as follows:

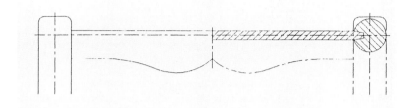

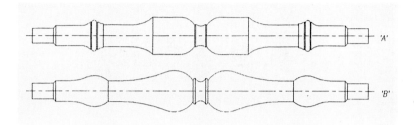

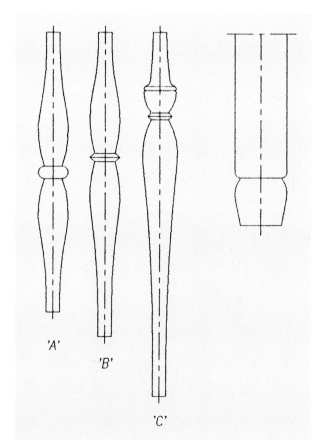

▲ Fig 19.1 West Midlands wood seat.

▲ Fig 19.2 West Midlands stretchers.

◀ Fig 19.3 West Midlands spindle patterns and leg foot detail.

'A'

'B'

'C'

Corner Posts

1 Prepare bandsawn timber 50mm (2in) square for the three corner legs, and machine these to the dimensions given.

▶ Fig 19.4
General
arrangement of
corner chair.

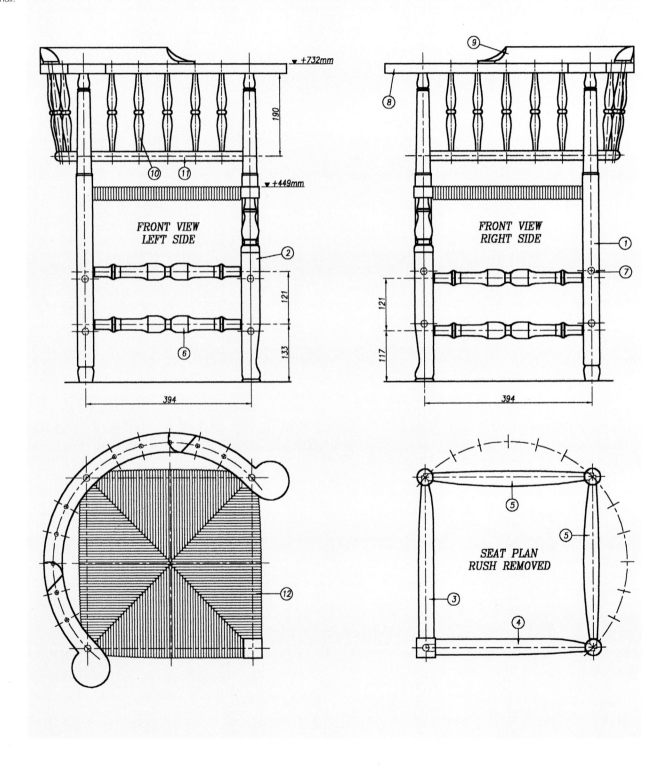

▼ +732mm

190

10   11

▼ +449mm

*FRONT VIEW
LEFT SIDE*

2

121

6

133

394

*FRONT VIEW
RIGHT SIDE*

9

8

1

7

121

117

394

12

5

5

*SEAT PLAN
RUSH REMOVED*

3

4

◄ Fig 19.5 Front leg, corner post and stretcher details.

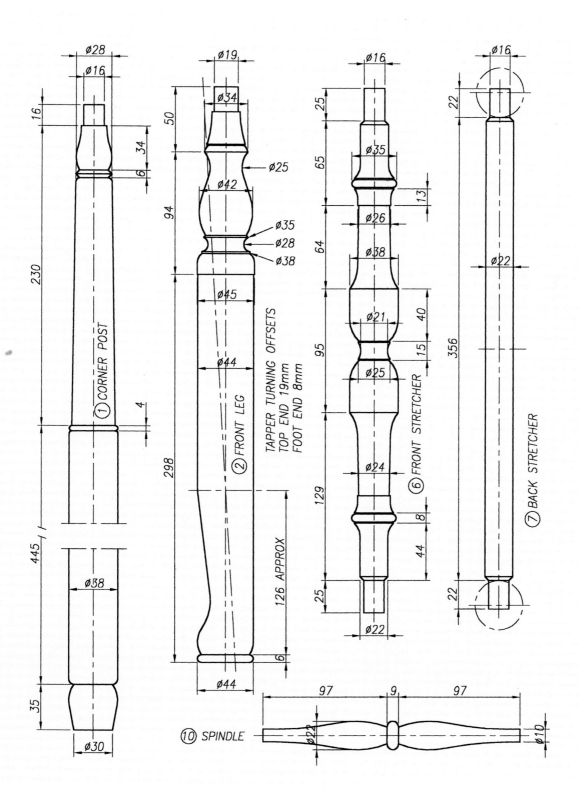

Ø28

Ø16

16

34

6

230

4

① CORNER POST

445

Ø38

35

Ø30

Ø19

Ø34

50

Ø25

94

Ø42

Ø35
Ø28
Ø38

Ø45

298

Ø44

② FRONT LEG

TAPPER TURNING OFFSETS
TOP END 19mm
FOOT END 8mm

126 APPROX

6

Ø44

⑩ SPINDLE

97   9   97

Ø22   Ø10

Ø16

25

Ø35

65

13

Ø26

64

Ø38

Ø21

95

40

15

Ø25

129

Ø24

⑥ FRONT STRETCHER

8

44

25

Ø22

Ø16

22

356

Ø22

⑦ BACK STRETCHER

22

▶ Fig 19.6 Seat rail and armrest details.

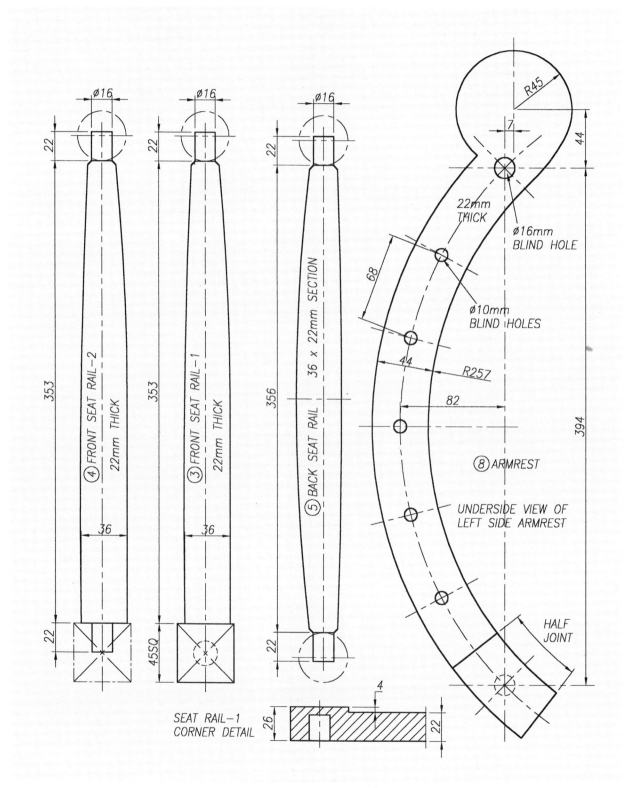

Ø16

22

353

④ FRONT SEAT RAIL – 2
22mm THICK

36

22

Ø16

22

353

③ FRONT SEAT RAIL – 1
22mm THICK

36

45SQ

SEAT RAIL – 1
CORNER DETAIL

Ø16

22

356

⑤ BACK SEAT RAIL   36 x 22mm SECTION

22

26   4   22

R45

7

44

22mm THICK

Ø16mm BLIND HOLE

68

Ø10mm BLIND HOLES

44

R257

82

394

⑧ ARMREST

UNDERSIDE VIEW OF LEFT SIDE ARMREST

HALF JOINT

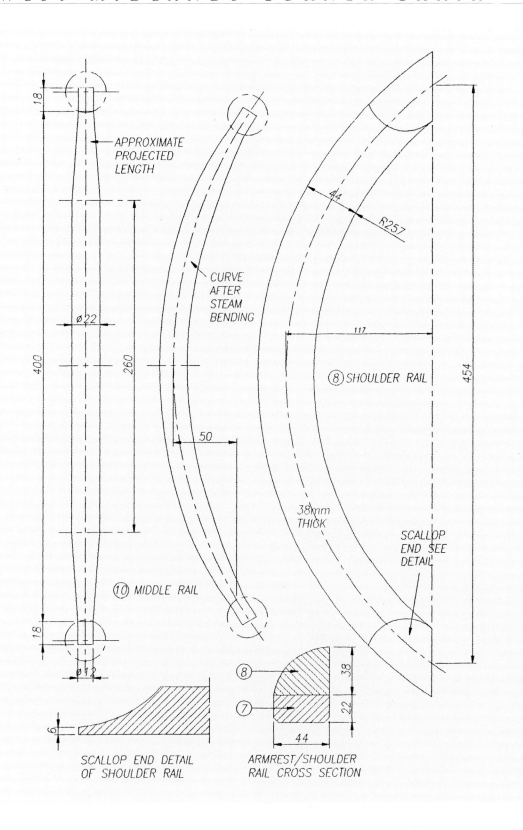

APPROXIMATE
PROJECTED
LENGTH

18

⌀22

400

260

CURVE
AFTER
STEAM
BENDING

50

⑩ MIDDLE RAIL

18

⌀12

44

R257

117

⑧ SHOULDER RAIL

454

38mm
THICK

SCALLOP
END SEE
DETAIL

6

SCALLOP END DETAIL
OF SHOULDER RAIL

⑧

⑦

38

22

44

ARMREST/SHOULDER
RAIL CROSS SECTION

Front Leg

2 Cut material 50mm (2in) square for the front legs. These are of cabriole form with a narrow pad foot. The offset turning technique for machining these is given in Chapter 2 (see page 12). The legs taper down quite sharply over quite a short length from below the bottom stretcher, so the offset axis for turning the taper is more angled. Machine the leg first on its true axis, and then offset this approximately 19mm (³/₄ in) at the top end, and 8mm (⁵/₁₆ in) at the foot for tapering down. Arrange the offset so the pad foot is set at 45 degrees towards the corner. With a large offset at the headstock end you need to keep the lathe speed down and make sure you leave sufficient material for the drive centre to grip the wood, i.e. do not be too eager to trim the leg end down ready for parting off, but leave this until later. The null point where both axes of rotation are concentric is roughly at the level of the bottom stretcher. If desired the neck of the taper can be undercut slightly on the back, so the edge is not straight at the bottom end when viewed from the side.

Stretchers

3 Prepare bandsawn material for the eight stretchers and woodturn these according to the measurements given.

Seat Rails

4 Prepare stock material for the seat rails, mount on the lathe to machine the end dowels, then bandsaw these to shape and chamfer the edges where the rush is wound round. Note that one of the front seat rails needs to be slightly thicker than the other to form a raised square pad end. This is so that the rush seat has an edge which it can butt up to at the corner, and which will be roughly level with the surface of the rush when weaving is completed.

Armrest

5 The armrest is made from two pieces of timber cut to a radius, and half jointed in the middle. Initially cut the two halves only roughly to shape leaving an excess of, say, 10mm (³/₈ in) all round. Leave the blanks to one side for a few days, to relieve any internal stresses which might cause the curvature to change slightly. Wood movement can be especially troublesome on timber which is cut to a curved rather than straight form. If you fail to do this you may find yourself struggling later, when trying to position the armrests over the corner posts and marry the middle half joint together.

6 Having stress-relieved the blanks, trace the armrest pattern on to these including the hole positions for the corner posts (1) and spindles (10). Finish cutting these to shape either by hand or machine. If you wish, you could use router techniques to do this. You can either make templates, and use the router fitted with a straight cutter/guide bearing to follow the pattern, or you could mount the router on a radius arm. Use the 16mm (⁵/₈ in) holes drilled for the end posts, fitted with short dowels as a register to hold the template to the work (Fig 19.9). If you do not have a router table, double-sided tape works quite well to stick the armrest to the bench whilst routing, provided this is done with caution. Drill out the intermediate holes for the back spindles (10).

7 Prepare planed timber of appropriate thickness for the shoulder rail (9). Mark out the profile, and initially cut it roughly to shape to fit over the armrests. As for the armrest, leave it aside for a few days for the timber to stress relieve itself.

Spindle Back

8 Prepare bandsawn stock for the 10 back spindles and machine these according to Fig 19.5.

▶ Fig 19.8
Corner seat rail
detail showing
raised end pad.

▶▶ Fig 19.9
Finished routed
armrests.

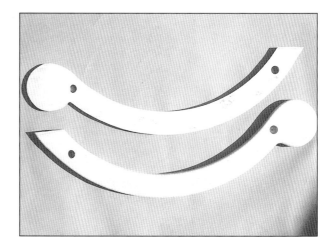

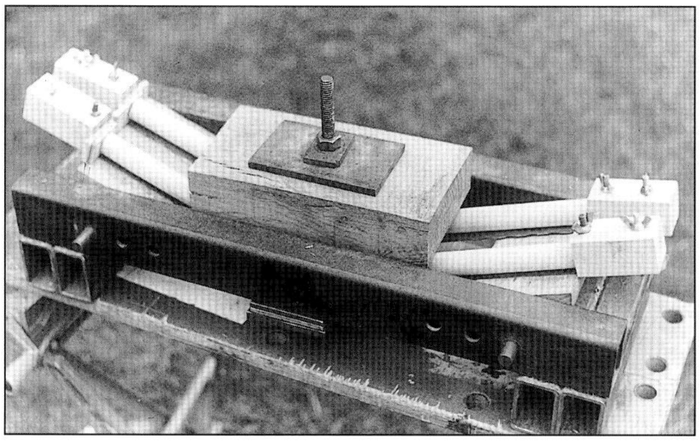

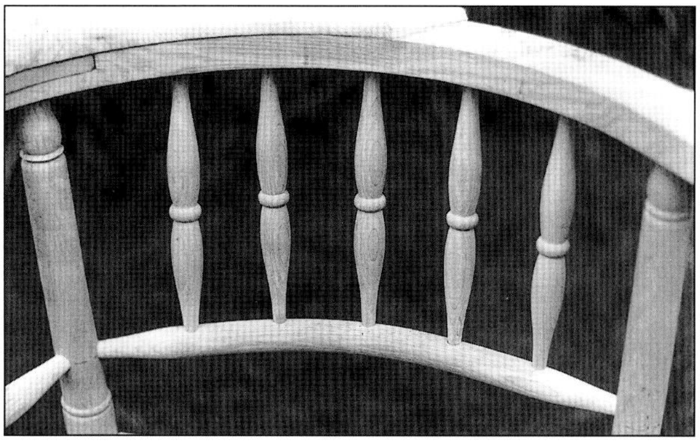

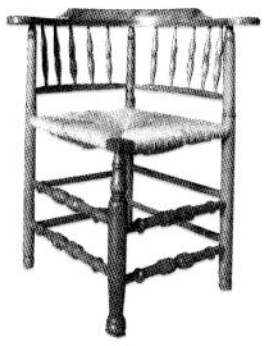

◂◂ *Fig 19.10 Steam bending middle rail.*

◂ *Fig 19.11 Assembling the chair.*

9 Cut material for the two middle rails (11) and woodturn these according to Fig 19.7. These items are steam bent. Follow the guidelines for steam bending in Chapter 4 (see page 23). Note the comments regarding the wood condition to minimise the risk of tension failure. When bent and set, drill the 10mm ($^{3}/_{8}$in) blind holes ready for the back spindles (10). Note that these rails do not need to be bent fully to the curvature of the armrest.

Slat Back

10 As an alternative to the spindle backs you could fit a single slat on either side. If you decide to do this, I would suggest that you chose a slat pattern as in Fig 11.2(C). This was a style used by West Midlands chair makers.

Leg and Corner Post Holes

11 Use the 'V' jig (see page 17) to drill the holes in the front leg and corner posts. These are all 90 degrees, except those for the middle rail (11) which are angled accordingly. For these, trace the pattern onto a piece of paper and measure the angle.

First Assembly

12 Commence assembly by fitting together one back frame, items (1), (5), (7), and (11), and one front frame, items (1), (2), (3) and (6). Link these together with the remaining profiled/plain stretchers, seat rails and the second middle rail (11).

13 Add the spindles (10) and the armrests (8). Check the armrests half joint neatly together over the back corner post dowel end. Lay the shoulder rail on top of the armrest, and trace the edge profile underneath. Remove and trim the shoulder rail edges so it fits the armrest exactly, then scallop down the ends as indicated.

Finishing

14 Dismantle to do as much prefinishing work as practicably possible, staining, sealing and polishing the surfaces as appropriate.

Final Assembly

15 Reassemble and glue the chair together following through steps 12 and 13 again. Wipe off any excess glue with a damp cloth. Finish polishing any surfaces needing attention.

Rush Seat

16 Follow the guidelines in Chapter 5 (see page 31) for rush seating. As an alternative and for a quicker result, use seagrass.

Parts List

Item	Description	No	Material	Dimensions
1	Corner post	3	Ash	50mm sq x 760mm long (2in sq x 30in long)
2	Front leg	1	Ash	50mm sq x 470mm long (2in sq x $18\frac{1}{2}$in long)
3	Front seat rail (1)	2	Ash	50 x 25 x 450mm long (2 x 1 x $17\frac{3}{4}$in long)
4	Front seat rail (2)	2	Ash	40 x 22 x 450mm long ($1\frac{5}{8}$ x $\frac{7}{8}$ x $17\frac{3}{4}$in long)
5	Back seat rail	2	Ash	40 x 22 x 440mm long ($1\frac{5}{8}$ x $\frac{7}{8}$ x $17\frac{1}{2}$ in long)
6	Front stretcher	2	Ash	45mm sq x 450mm long ($1\frac{3}{4}$in sq x $17\frac{3}{4}$in long)
7	Back stretcher	2	Ash	28mm sq x 450mm long ($1\frac{1}{8}$in sq x $17\frac{3}{4}$in long)
8	Armrest	2	Ash	155 x 22 x 540mm long ($6\frac{1}{8}$ x $\frac{7}{8}$ x $21\frac{1}{2}$in long)
9	Shoulder rail	1	Ash	140 x 38 x 520mm long ($5\frac{1}{2}$ x $1\frac{1}{2}$ x $20\frac{1}{2}$in long)
10	Back spindle	10	Ash	28mm sq x 170mm long ($1\frac{1}{8}$in sq x $6\frac{3}{4}$in long)
11	Middle rail	2	Ash	28mm sq x 450mm long ($1\frac{1}{8}$in sq x $17\frac{3}{4}$in long)
12	Rush seat		Rush	1 bolt – sufficient for 2 seats

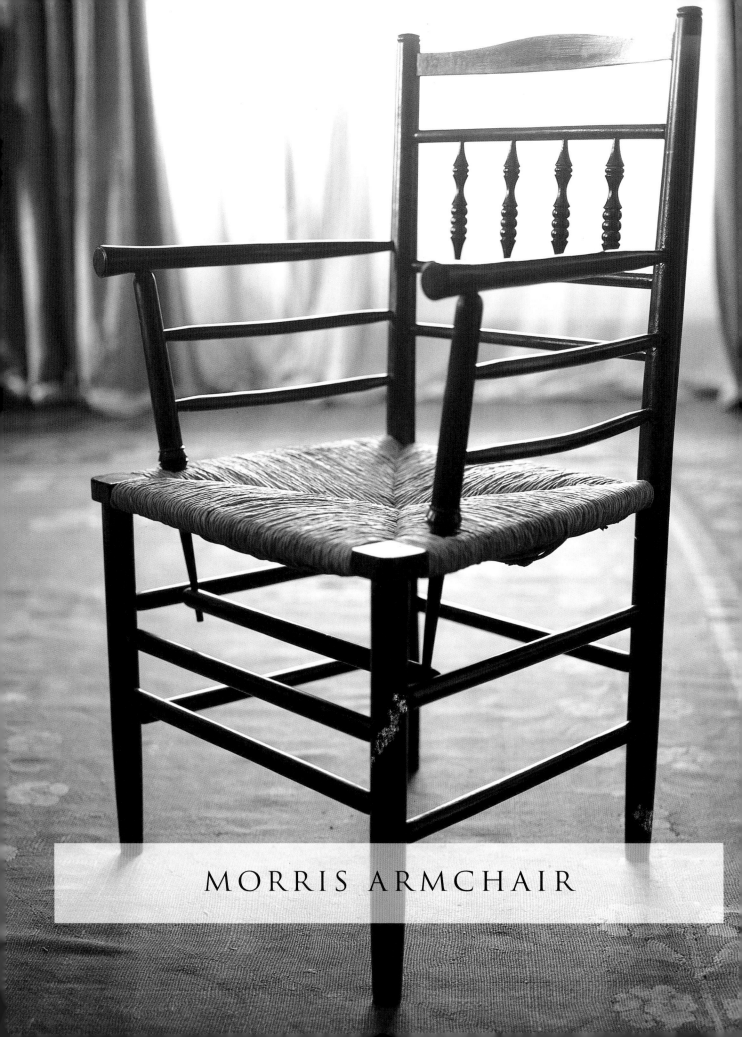

MORRIS ARMCHAIR

The Arts and Craft Movement of the Victorian era was evolved by many artists, writers and crafts people. The most renowned of these was William Morris (1834–1896) who is regarded by many as the founding father of the Movement. Born at Walthamstow and educated at Marlborough, his childhood days at school were apparently not happy ones. As he matured, he began to reject the everyday humdrum pressures of work and technology, and turned instead to the arts. Primarily an artist, and later a socialist, he had a vision to create objects with an artistic appearance. His company, Morris, Marshall, Faulkner & Co, started in 1861, known as the 'Firm', produced objects on which he could apply decoration, such as wallpapers, fabrics and printed manuscripts. Morris drew much of his inspiration from art galleries, and was a frequent visitor to the Victoria and Albert Museum. Though his products were of high quality, it took some time before they were accepted by other manufacturers and society. He is probably best remembered for his wall hangings, and especially the wallpaper he created called 'Trellis'. A quotation attributable to William Morris is 'Have nothing in your house which you do not know to be useful, or believe to be beautiful'. Today a century later we are witnessing a revival of interest in products inspired by him.

WILLIAM MORRIS CHAIRS

Among the many things produced by William Morris's company were ebonised rush-bottomed chairs in a style which he called the 'Sussex' range. A feature of Morris chairs is the slender nature of the rails and stretchers, many of which were bent to a shallow curve. The spindle work on the back also had tapered, bead and cove shapes, which once seen are instantly recognisable. Another unique characteristic was the way the front armrest was sometimes supported, not on an extension of the front leg, but by a separate turned spindle. This had a long tapered end below the seat, and was set slightly angled through the side rail terminating in a hole in a stretcher beneath.

ARMCHAIR DESIGN

The design here is measured from an original Morris chair dating from about 1860–1890. It has tapered front legs and back posts, linked with pairs of stretchers to the front and side, and a single stretcher behind. The back features a shallow arched slat, below which are three lightly bent rails incorporating a row of four bead-form spindles. The curved armrests are carried by taper-ended supports, which slope characteristically inwards through a hole in the seat rail, the end fitting into a cross stretcher below. The chair is made of beech with a black ebonised finish, and is rush seated.

CONSTRUCTION

The techniques needed to make this chair are woodturning, joinery, steam bending and rush weaving for the seat. The parts requiring bending are the back posts (2), slat (9), middle rails (10), armrests (12) and the armrest side rails (14). With the exception of the armrest, the bent parts generally have a shallow curvature, so can be steam bent without problems, and air-dried timber should be adequate. With regard to the choice of wood, and bearing in mind the ebonised finish, there are other close-grained timbers you could use besides beech, such as apple, pear and cherry. I have used pear in the past, but I found it would not steam bend as easily as beech. The general arrangement is given in Fig 20.1 and details of the parts in Figs 20.2 and 20.3. The order of work is as follows.

Front Legs and Back Posts

1   Prepare 45mm (1³/₄ in) square stock for the front legs and back posts, and woodturn these to the measurements given. The front legs and back posts taper towards the bottom, and the latter tapers also from the seat upwards.

Stretchers

2   Bandsaw material 28mm (1¹/₈ in) square for the stretchers (6) and (7), and the cross stretcher (8). Approximate lengths for these are given on the drawings, though these may vary slightly, depending on the final form of the back posts. You may thus have to take local check measurements, and it may be better to machine those for the sides at a later stage after other parts have been steam bent, and prior to assembly.

Seat Rails

3   Prepare planed material of appropriate cross section, machine the end spigots, then bandsaw the rails to the profile given. To take account of the rush thickness, and provide a firm edge for the rush weave to butt up to, the front rail has raised square pad corners (see Fig 20.2). On the side seat rails, the holes where the armrest supports pass through are not a tight fit, but are enlarged slightly to permit rush seating later.

Back Rails, Spindles and Armrest

4   Cut 25mm (1in) square stock for the three middle rails (10) and armrest side rails (14), and woodturn these to 16mm (⁵/₈ in) diameter as shown in Fig 20.3. Similarly prepare material for the armrest (12), armrest support (13) and spindles (11), and machine these as indicated.

Back Slat

5   Prepare planed material 6mm (¹/₄ in) thick for the back slat. Steam this for 20 minutes, and bend to a shallow profile under

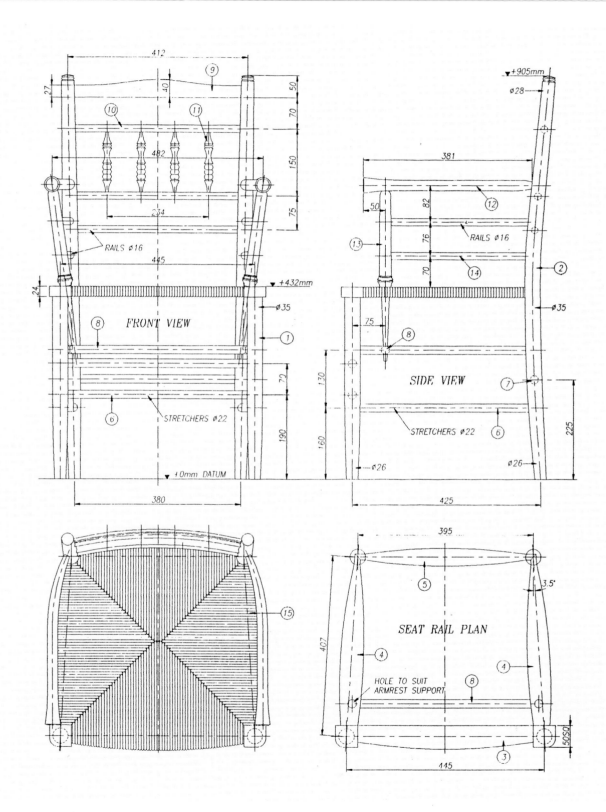

▶ Fig. 20.1
General
arrangement of
William Morris
armchair.

FRONT VIEW

RAILS Ø16

STRETCHERS Ø22

SIDE VIEW

RAILS Ø16

STRETCHERS Ø22

SEAT RAIL PLAN

HOLE TO SUIT
ARMREST SUPPORT

◀ Fig. 20.2 Front leg and seat rail details.

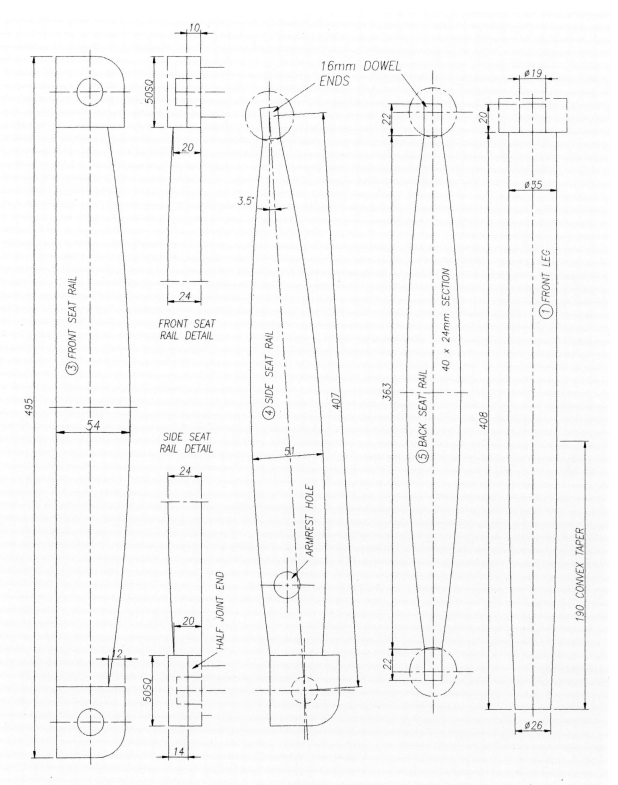

16mm DOWEL ENDS

Ø19

Ø35

10

50SQ

20

24

FRONT SEAT RAIL DETAIL

③ FRONT SEAT RAIL

495

54

22

20

3.5°

④ SIDE SEAT RAIL

407

⑤ BACK SEAT RAIL

40 x 24mm SECTION

363

408

① FRONT LEG

190 CONVEX TAPER

SIDE SEAT RAIL DETAIL

24

20

HALF JOINT END

50SQ

2

14

51

ARMREST HOLE

22

Ø26

▸ *Fig. 20.3 Slat, stretcher and armrest details.*

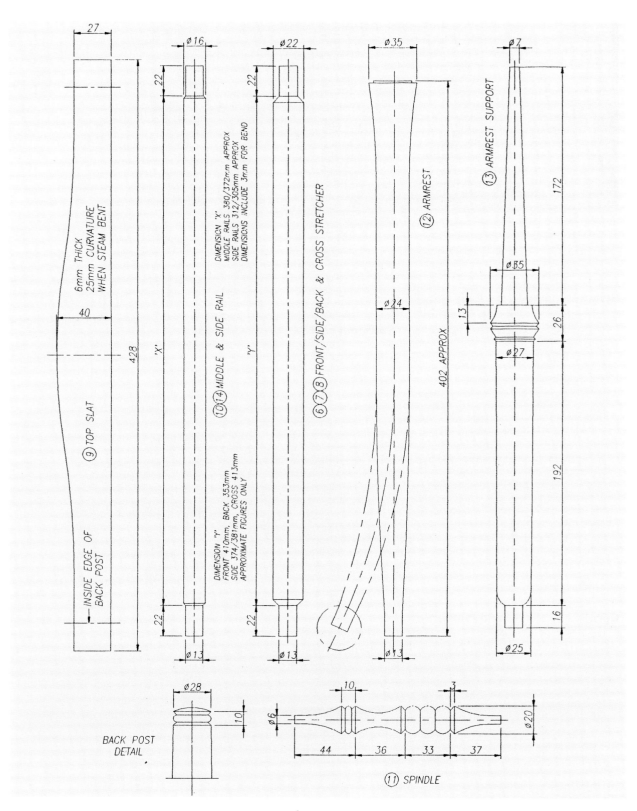

27

Ø16

Ø22

Ø35

Ø7

22

22

6mm THICK
25mm CURVATURE
WHEN STEAM BENT

DIMENSION 'Y'
MIDDLE RAILS 380/372mm APPROX
SIDE RAILS 312/305mm APPROX
DIMENSIONS INCLUDE 3mm FOR BEND

⑬ ARMREST SUPPORT

172

40

'X'

'Y'

⑫ ARMREST

428

Ø24

Ø35

13

26

⑨ TOP SLAT

⑩⑭ MIDDLE & SIDE RAIL

⑥⑦⑧ FRONT/SIDE/BACK & CROSS STRETCHER

402 APPROX

Ø27

192

DIMENSION 'Y'
FRONT 410mm, BACK 353mm
SIDE 374/381mm, CROSS 413mm
APPROXIMATE FIGURES ONLY

INSIDE EDGE OF
BACK POST

22

22

16

Ø13

Ø13

Ø13

Ø25

Ø28

10

3

10

Ø6

Ø20

BACK POST
DETAIL

44

36

33

37

⑪ SPINDLE

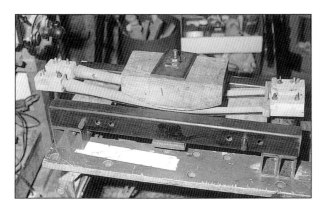

◄◄ Fig 20.4
Bending the
armrest.

◄ Fig 20.5
Armrest support
details.

◄ Fig 20.6
Assembly of chair
back.

the slat press. The curvature is approximately 20mm (³/₄ in), so the mould curve needs to be about 38mm (1¹/₂ in) to allow for spring back.

Steam Bending Posts, Rails and Stretchers

6 Use the post bending jig (see page 26), to bend the chair back posts. About 1¹/₄ hours' steaming should be sufficient. The posts are bent to a fairly shallow curve, so limit this by inserting packing under the foot or top end of the post whilst screwing down. The legs are shorter than others, so the screw jack position will have to be moved nearer towards the hump block.

7 Use the spindle bending jig (see page 27) to bend the middle rails (10), armrests (12) and armrest side rails (14). The curvature for the rails is approximately 20mm (³/₄ in). You might experience problems with bending the armrest. I found it best to machine this with a long spigot end where it fits into the back post, and to bend this eccentrically towards the back on the spindle bending jig. This will move the curve towards the back where it is needed. I also found it necessary to fit a mini-steel strap to minimise tension failure on the outside whilst bending it.

Corner Post Holes and Mortises

8 Use the 'V' jig (see page 17) to drill the holes in the front legs, and the two-way sliding/tilt jig (see page 18) for the holes in the back posts. The holes for the side seat rails and stretchers are offset 4 degrees either side. The back posts are tapered in approximately 1 degree, but it is not really necessary to tilt the drill table by this amount.

9 The mortise slots for the slat (9), and the holes for the middle rails (10) are approximately 10 degrees off centre set towards the back about 3mm (¹/₈ in). These assume a bend of 20mm (³/₄ in). As a check, trace the edge of the slat on to a piece of paper and measure the angle before you start. Cut the mortise holes by chain drilling and then clean these up.

10 The armrest angle into the back post as shown on the drawings in plan is about 24 degrees. This is one angle you may have to experiment with. If in doubt, trace it out and measure it first.

11 The armrest support (13) is angled about 8 degrees outwards.

▸ *Fig 20.7 Rush seating round the armrest.*

First Assembly

12 Fit together the components for the front and back frames individually and check these are square and without wind. Then offer these frames together with the side seat rails and stretchers, also fitting in the cross stretcher (8) as you go.

13 Drop in the armrest support (13) through the holes in the seat rails and cross stretcher, and check the fitting of these. Finally, add on the armrests (12) and the rails (14). To fit these, you may have to withdraw the back frame slightly, to let the dowel ends into their respective holes. Ensure that the chair now stands squarely.

Finishing

14 Dismantle the chair to do as much prefinishing as possible. The chair has a silk-effect ebonised finish. To do this first colour the parts with a black oil stain with a dash of 880 ammonia added to help drive this into the grain. Next fill the grain to seal the surfaces, and then apply French polish. For the latter you can use a ready-made black ebony polish, or use French polish either with added spirit black or lamp black. One of the troublesome areas for obtaining a jet black finish are wood items with sharp edges, such as seat rails, where you do not want to cut through the polish and reveal the bare wood beneath. Make sure these are all suitably smoothed over. To produce the final eggshell finish, use a soft brush dipped in pumice powder and draw this along the surfaces. Lastly as an alternative you could paint the chair a matt black and wax this afterwards. If you choose this option, you can wait till after the chair is glued up to do this.

Final Assembly

15 Re-assemble the chair applying glue to the various dowel connections. Follow through steps 12 and 13 to rebuild the chair. Wipe off any excess glue with a damp cloth. Finish any surfaces needing treatment.

Rush Seat

16 Follow the guidelines for rush seating as given in Chapter 5 (see page 31). One problem area is the point where the armrest supports (13) pass through the holes in the seat side rails. As mentioned earlier the holes are left over-large, to allow you to rush the rail on the outside as well as the inside (see Fig 20.7). Otherwise the rush material would be bunched in an unsightly way around the armrest support. One bolt of rush should be adequate for this chair.

PARTS LIST

Item	Description	No	Material	Dimensions
1	Front leg	2	Beech	45mm sq x 470mm long (1¾ in sq x 18½ in long)
2	Back post	2	Beech	45mm sq x 950mm long (1¾ in sq x 37½ in long)
3	Front seat rail	1	Beech	54 x 25 x 520mm long (2⅛ x 1 x 20½ in long)
4	Side seat rail	2	Beech	54 x 25 x 450mm long (2⅛ x 1 x 17¾ in long)
5	Back seat rail	1	Beech	40 x 25 x 430mm long (1⅝ x 1 x 17in long)
6	Front/side stretcher	6	Beech	28mm sq x 460mm long (1⅛ in sq x 18⅛ in long)
7	Back stretcher	1	Beech	28mm sq x 420mm long (1⅛in sq x 16 in long)
8	Cross stretcher	1	Beech	28mm sq x 460mm long (1⅛ in sq x 18⅛ in long)
9	Top slat	1	Beech	45 x 6 x 450mm long (1¾ x ¼ x 17¾ in long)
10	Middle rail	2	Beech	22mm sq x 450mm long (⅞ in sq x 17¾ in long)
11	Back spindle	4	Beech	25mm sq x 170mm long (1in sq x 6¾ in long)
12	Armrest	2	Beech	42mm sq x 430mm long (1⅝ in sq x 17in long)
13	Armrest support	2	Beech	42mm sq x 420mm long (1⅝ in sq x 16½ in long)
14	Armrest side rail	4	Beech	22mm sq x 360mm long (⅞ in sq x 14¼ in long)
15	Rush seat	1	English rush	1 bolt – enough for 2 seats

BIBLIOGRAPHY

CHAIR HISTORY
Dr B.D. Cotton, *The English Regional Chair*
Marjorie Filbee, *Dictionary of Country Furniture*
Nancy Goyne Evans, *American Windsor Chairs*
Ralph & Terry Kovel, *American Country Furniture 1780–1875*
Charles R. Muller & Timothy D. Rieman, *The Shaker Chair*

CHAIR MAKING
Mike Abbott, *Green Woodwork*, GMC Publications,
Herbert Edlin, *Woodland Crafts in Britain*, David & Charles,
Harold Hart (editor), *Chairs Through the Ages*,
Jack Hill, *Country Chair Making*
John G. Shea, *Making Authentic Shaker Furniture*

WOOD BENDING
W.C. Stevens & N. Turner, *Wood Bending Handbook*, Forest
     Products Research Laboratory
Fine Woodworking on Bending Wood, The Taunton Press
Building Research Establishment – Technical Notes
Selecting ash by inspection (No.54)
The movement of timbers (No.38)
The bending of solid timber (No.52)
The strength of timber (No.10)

CHAIR SEATING
Ricky Holdstock, *Seat Weaving*
K. Johnson, O.E. Barratt & M. Butcher, *Chair Seating: Techniques in
     Cane, Rush Willow and Cords*
Robert J. McDonald, *Upholstery Repair and Restoration*

WOOD FINISHING
Frederick Oughton, *The Complete Manual of Wood Finishing*

INFORMATION DIRECTORY

SOCIETIES AND ASSOCIATIONS

United Kingdom

The Regional Furniture Society
Membership Secretary
The Trout House
Warrens Cross
Lechlade
Gloucestershire GL7 3DR
www.regionalfurnituresociety.com

The Furniture History Society
c/o The Furniture and Woodwork
    Collection
Victoria and Albert Museum
London SW7 2RL

Association of Woodturners of Great
Britain
Secretary
Hugh O'Neill
Myttons Craft Centre
Myttons Cottage
Boraston
Tenbury, Wells
Worcestershire HA6 1EW
Tel: 01584 810266
www.woodturners.co.uk

Northern Federation of Woodturning
    Groups
Ian Bartlett
13 Mort Lane
Tyldesley
Manchester M29 8BP
Tel/Fax: 0161 799 1733
www.woodturners.org.uk

United States

Shaker Heritage Society
Shaker Meeting House
Albany-Shaker Road
Albany
NY 12211
USA

Association of American Woodturners
www.woodturner.org

MUSEUMS

United Kingdom

High Wycombe Chair Museum
Castle Hill House
Priory Avenue
High Wycombe HP13 6PX
Tel: 01494 421895

The American Museum in Britain
Claverton Manor
Claverton Down
Bath BA2 7BD
Tel: 01225 460503

Towneley Art Gallery and Museum
Burnley
Lancashire BB11 3RQ
Tel: 01282 42413

Weald and Downland Open Air Museum
Singleton
Nr. Chichester
West Sussex PO18 0EU
Tel: 01243 811363
www.wealddown.co.uk

United States

Hancock Shaker Village
PO Box 898
Pittsfield
MA 01202

Canterbury Shaker Village
Canterbury
NH 03224
USA

MATERIALS AND SUPPLIERS

United Kingdom

English Rush Seating

Felicity Irons
Struttle End Farm
Old Ways Road
Ravensden
Bedfordshire MK44 2RD
Tel: 01234 771980

Country Chairmen
Home Farm
Ardington
Wantage
Oxon OX12 8PY
Tel: 01235 833614

Cane and Seagrass

Berrycraft
Acadia
Swansbrook Lane
Horam
Heathfield
East Sussex TN21 0LD
Tel: 01435 32383

**Shaker Seat Tape - Unbleached
Cotton Webbing**

David Bryant
4 Grassfield Way
Knutsford
Cheshire WA16 9AF
Tel/Fax: 01565 651681
www.craftdesign.co.uk

Plans
Workshop plans: A1 size plans of all the
chair designs in this book are available
from:

David Bryant
4 Grassfield Way
Knutsford
Cheshire WA16 9AF
Tel/Fax: 01565 651681
www.craftdesign.co.uk

~ INDEX ~